Renee Fisher wants you to know that forgiving those who have caused you pain is the most Christlike decision you will ever make, and the one most likely to set you free from your past and heal your damaged emotions.

—**Dr. Neil T. Anderson,** Founder and President
Emeritus of Freedom in Christ Ministries

Forgiveness is one of God's most powerful healing processes. When we fail to forgive we are in bondage to our past. *Forgiving Others, Forgiving Me* can be a liberating read.

—**Josh McDowell,** author of *The Unshakable Truth* and
New Evidence That Demands a Verdict

Renee Fisher graciously shares how to find and extend forgiveness to others—including yourself. Use this book to help you find your second (or seventy-seventh) chance.

—**Mike Foster,** People of the Second Chance

We're so proud of Renee, a Christian Writers Guild alum who is using her skills to tell her story to advance the kingdom.

—**Jerry B. Jenkins**, New York Times bestselling author

Infused with solid biblical truth and gut-real stories, author Renee Fisher helps us all find the forgiveness that seems so elusive in this vengeance-filled society. Oh the beauty of letting go of bitterness!

—**Mary DeMuth,** author of *The Wall Around Your Heart* and *Everything*

I have taught on forgiveness, reconciliation, and redemption for over 30 years and it continues to be one of the most challenging topics for people to deal with. In this helpful and interactive book, Renee Fisher helps the reader process the hurt, pain, and confusion to discover God's truth and a path to freedom.

—**Pam Farrel,** author of *Men Are Like Waffles—Women Are Like Spaghetti*

Forgiving Others, Forgiving Me is like cleaning the clutter out of the closet of your heart. With candidness and hope, Renee encourages each of us to take a look at what needs to be dusted off and given away. Given to whom? Given to God, who honors our transparency and works whatever weighs us down into the fabric of our lives with a fresh start.

—**Marcia Ramsland,** speaker and author of *Simplify Your Life*

With a strong voice that doesn't shy away from the hard questions, Renee Fisher writes with wisdom about some of the best and hardest ways we experience God's grace. You can expect to be comforted by her honesty while challenged by her insightful teaching on applying God's Word in our lives. She makes me want to seek and be changed by God—and nothing is more encouraging than that.

—**Nicole Unice,** author of *She's Got Issues*

The Devotional Diva does it again. Deeply rooted in God's Word and grace, *Forgiving Others, Forgiving Me* will bring hope to the hearts of many. I encourage all who may be trapped by unforgiveness to have the courage to open these pages and explore the truth that will set you free.

—**Crystal Renaud,** author of *Dirty Girls Come Clean*

For so many people, the idea of forgiving themselves keeps them from accepting the utmost forgiveness of Jesus. With a topic that touches everyone's lives (whether or not we like to admit it), Renee will be a cheerleader and mentor in the journey of forgiveness and a more fulfilling Christian walk.

—**Sarah Francis Martin,** author of *Stress Point*

Renee Fisher understands the issue of forgiveness cannot be resolved with superficial platitudes. Her transparency in sharing her own story gives credence to the hope she offers for those shackled by chains of unforgiveness. This book is not merely an intellectual exercise, but a journey of heart and soul that will free readers to fulfill God's purpose for their lives.

—**Ava Pennington,** author of *Daily Reflections on the Names of God*

Renee successfully uses Scripture and real-life stories to demonstrate both why forgiveness is necessary and how it can be accomplished. Readers will also have opportunities to reflect on their own brokenness and broken relationships through Renee's creative journaling prompts.

—**Lisa Velthouse,** author of *Craving Grace*

True to form, Renee Fisher tackles difficult subjects with a healthy portion of grace. *Forgiving Others, Forgiving Me* is a great resource for young people who have experienced heartbreak but haven't yet been able to find forgiveness for themselves or others.

—**Allison Vesterfelt,** author of *Packing Light*

Renee Fisher has written a powerful book on the most important issue every human being wrestles with. Mined from her own personal experiences, her exuberant personality and fresh approach overflows each page. This book is liberating!

—**Ray Bentley,** Pastor of Maranatha Chapel, San Diego

Renee Fisher takes the reader on a journey of confronting and loving oneself, those around her, and most importantly, God. Inspirational, practical, and so very helpful!

—**Jennie Gillespie,** President, San Diego Christian Writers Guild

Rather than focusing on your painful past, Renee Fisher invites you to confront and conquer the deeply rooted emotions that draw you farther from the Lord. Forgiveness is much easier to talk about than it is to put into place, but Renee will remind you that it is all worthwhile as you find reconciliation in the unconditional grace of Jesus.

—**Lisa Copen,** founder and director of Rest Ministries

It's easy to become stuck in shame from past mistakes and stuck in resentment from past wounds. Grab this book and take on the life-altering challenge of forgiving others and yourself.

—**Tyler Braun,** author of *Why Holiness Matters*

RENEE FISHER

Forgiving Others, Forgiving Me

HARVEST HOUSE PUBLISHERS
EUGENE, OREGON

Cover by Knail, Salem, Oregon

Published in association with the literary agency of Credo Communications, LLC, Grand Rapids, Michigan, www.credocommunications.net

Cover photos © plainpicture / Fancy Images; Hemera / Thinkstock; iStockphoto / Thinkstock

Back cover author photo © www.vilchissquared.com

FORGIVING OTHERS, FORGIVING ME
Copyright © 2013 by Renee Fisher
Published by Harvest House Publishers
Eugene, Oregon 97402
www.harvesthousepublishers.com

Library of Congress Cataloging-in-Publication Data
    Fisher, Renee, 1982-
    Forgiving others, forgiving me / Renee Fisher.
        pages cm
    ISBN 978-0-7369-4727-5 (pbk.)
    ISBN 978-0-7369-4728-2 (eBook)
    1. Forgiveness–Religious aspects–Christianity. 2. Spiritual life–Christianity. 3. Christian life.
    4. Forgiveness of sin. 5. Spirituality. I. Title.
    BV4647.F55F58 2013
    234'.5—dc23
                                                                        2012044764

Printed in the United States of America

        13 14 15 16 17 18 19 20 21 / VP-CD / 10 9 8 7 6 5 4 3 2 1

To LaRae, Barb, and Kathleen
for the opportunity to resurrect the dream to tell my story.
I am in your debt.

Table of Contents

Forgiving Me: A Self-Portrait

I had been writing in my journal every night since December of 1997 when my life fell apart. I wrote to overcome the biggest fear of all: *myself*. I addressed each journal entry to God, hoping He would hear and answer my prayers for healing. And I needed healing. My skin was covered in rashes, the medication had caused me to gain one hundred pounds as a teenager, I dealt with crippling bouts of anxiety, and I lost my first love. And God did heal me…in a *big* way. Scriptures flooded my journal. Prayers came spilling in and healing cascaded like a tidal wave over me as I wrote each night. God came alive as I wrote to Him, and it was there in my journal that I found what I was searching for—*forgiveness*.

My shyness as a writer was no longer an issue. I kept writing to find the comfort of consistency in my pen and journal. My journal was my escape from the busy world. Writing quickly grew into the quiet obsession at the end of my day. I allowed myself to write a daily self-portrait. I wrote to be honest with myself and with God—honest about the sorrow, the ecstasy, and even the mundane. Each self-portrait included a different name—*Visionary. Dreamer. Fearful. Lovely. Afraid. Pure.* The names helped me to take my mind off what was going wrong to see the beauty and find forgiveness from God that I so desperately needed. There was no longer anyone standing in my way. Not even me.

Before You Begin

Did you ever think you were meant for something BIG? Maybe you wanted to climb Mount Everest, have a baby, or finally finish that college degree. Instead of achieving your goals, something *bigger* happened…and you were robbed of the life you dreamed.

Overcoming *is* possible!

There is freedom in Christ from your past hurts, present circumstances, and future fears.

Every chapter in this book includes real quotes from people like you, encouraging words to guide you through the healing process, and discussion questions with journaling space. Before starting this book, I urge you to consider getting a Bible study or small group together so you don't have to go through this process alone. You will find group discussion questions in the back of the book.

May you too find freedom in the journey from pain to *purpose*!

PART 1

MOLDED

You have everything backward!

You treat the potter as a lump of clay.

Does a book say to its author,

"He didn't write a word of me"?

Does a meal say to the woman who cooked it,

"She had nothing to do with this"?

ISAIAH 29:16 MSG

CHAPTER 1

Number-One Fear

How is it possible that choosing to forgive someone can actually backfire? You finally muster up the courage to come face-to-face with the person who hurt you...and you're the one who walks away hurt?

Maybe it's because you can *only* control how you act, react, and respond.

Maybe it's because you were *ready* to let things go, but the other person wasn't.

We have the idea that forgiveness takes two people, but really it only takes one—and that's you!

Imagine with me for a second that you're sitting in a movie theater minding your own business. You indulge in a large Coke and popcorn to share with friends. This day couldn't come at a better time—the week has taken its toll and you're just so glad it's the weekend. Not to mention you enjoy watching Christian Bale don a Batman costume. Yes, his voice is weird when he speaks as Batman, but who cares? You just want to be entertained.

Maybe you even send out a tweet or tag yourself on Facebook to say something like, "Movie starts in two minutes!" Then you settle in to enjoy the movie. But before you can take another swig of refreshing cola you see a shadow burst through the door and *bang*—live sound effects. At first you think the theater went above and beyond, and then you're ducking behind people screaming for their lives. Bullets are flying everywhere and the person next to you gets hit in the arm and the nose. You don't even have time to think.

What in the world is going on? And where is God in all of this?

The event I just described actually happened. A man wearing riot gear and carrying a few high-powered rifles terrorized a midnight showing of *The Dark Knight Rises* in Aurora, Colorado, in July 2012. I didn't even mention the tear gas he threw first to make people believe it was special effects. He killed twelve people and wounded fifty-eight more.

How is anyone supposed to forgive *that* guy?

Some people made it out alive and others didn't. It's hard to imagine how long it will take for the victims and the families of those wounded to forgive the man responsible. It goes against every human instinct to forgive someone who had no regard for age, sex, or race. He killed in cold blood.

Number-One Fear

It is no surprise that people fear things like public speaking or going to the dentist. But there's another fear we don't hear talked about as much. Forgiveness.

We'd rather not think about forgiveness. Maybe your past is full of so many hurts and pains that trying to forgive others—including yourself—feels about as foolish as seeing daylight in a darkened tunnel.

My number-one future fear is my career. I want to be successful, yet it is hard to make your way up in this world, especially without giving up something you love. —Stacie, 22

But there's good news. You *can* trust God to lead you on the right path, even when you cannot help but look ahead and see fog—or tear gas.

Do you remember the story of Shadrach, Meshach, and Abednego? These three friends were commanded by King Nebuchadnezzar to fall down and worship an image he had made. "But if you do not worship it," he warned, "you will be thrown immediately into a blazing furnace. Then what god will be able to rescue you from my hand?" (Daniel 3:15).

The response from the three men simply stuns the king. They said,

> We do not need to defend ourselves before you in this matter. If we are thrown into the blazing furnace, the God we serve is able to deliver us from it, and he will deliver us from Your Majesty's hand. But even if he does not, we want you to know, Your Majesty, that we will not serve your gods or worship the image of gold you have set up (Daniel 3:16-18).

Fire reveals our true colors. King Nebuchadnezzar was so furious that he ordered the furnace to be heated seven times hotter than normal. It was so hot that the guards—the ones who were supposed to bind up the prisoners and throw them in the furnace—were incinerated in the heat. But Shadrach, Meshach, and Abednego were able to walk around in the furnace unharmed. God Himself saved those men.

So why didn't He save the people in that Colorado theater?

And what about all the rest of the murders around the world? What about the people who die in wars and famines? What about the people who are killed for believing in Jesus? Doesn't God care about *them?*

It takes time to see Jesus and let Him guide you through the smoke screen of life—through all the "what ifs"—including your number-one fear. Maybe you're afraid of death, or losing your health or job. Maybe you're afraid of being single forever. No matter *which* fears you're currently holding tight, remember this: Jesus is stronger than every one of them.

The Fear of Change

Fear makes you believe you are not good enough—like there's no way you'll make it out alive. Fear can masquerade as reality. We need to be challenged to change the way we think about fear. The first Bible verse I memorized was 2 Timothy 1:7. It says, "For the Spirit

God gave us does not make us timid, but gives us power, love, and self-discipline."

It's like the Jets versus the Sharks, the Bloods versus Crips, Good versus Evil in an invisible realm of divinity. We can't physically see it, but we see in Scripture multiple times that the battle always belongs to the Lord. —Bianca, 30

Maybe your mind can't help but wonder, What if this happens? What if that happens? We always go to the worst-case scenario. Second Corinthians 10:5 says that we must "demolish arguments and every pretension that sets itself up against the knowledge of God" and "take captive every thought to make it obedient to Christ." Can you imagine giving God all your fears? It would take all day! But that's exactly what God wants us to do. Your old way of living in denial is out. Bad things will continue to happen to people all over the world. The only thing you have control over is your mind. Your family can't change your thoughts. Your friends can't tell you what to think and say. Even Satan, who sets himself up against God and believers around the world, can't penetrate your mind. He can certainly plant seeds or bullets of fear, but it's up to you how you deal with them.

Instead of taking out your frustration at God, the one who is molding and shaping your life, take responsibility. It's time! You *must* face your fears and learn how to forgive with the help of the Holy Spirit. Don't be afraid to ask for the love and support of your friends and family.

Then move on!

"He really screwed up. Bad! Can I forgive? How can I do this right?" A gentle whisper inside you says, "It's impossible." But God screams, *"Yes!"*

It reminds me of the story of Elijah in 1 Kings 19. He had just called fire down from heaven and yet a threat from Queen Jezebel had him hightailing it out of there, hiding in a cave because he was too afraid to show his face. God had just struck down 450 prophets of Baal with fire from heaven—and Elijah had the audacity to despair? To tell God he'd given up?

Maybe you feel like wavering between right and wrong.

Maybe you want to keep your options open…just in case.

That's exactly what Elijah was up to…even though he had just asked the people, "How long will you waver between two opinions? If the LORD is God, follow him; but if Baal is God, follow him" (1 Kings 18:21).

I'm here to tell you that you need to let it go. Forgiveness is key. Maybe your fears are right—maybe you're not good or strong enough to forgive. But God is. Instead of indulging in your fears and hesitation any longer, choose reconciliation over despair, forgiveness over hatred, and freedom over bitterness. Jesus stands there waiting to help you take that first step of faith over the past. Let Him help you take away your number-one fear.

Remember in *Braveheart* when the Scots are lining up to face the British the first time? The British seemed like a fierce opponent and were far too superior. Many wanted to run. William Wallace when he went out to meet the envoy was asked, "And where do you think you're going?" "I'm going to pick a fight," he said. I love that…get in the adversary's face and pick that fight. You know you're going to win. —Trevor, 29

In His mercy, God appeared to Elijah. First a great and powerful wind announced His presence. The wind tore the mountains apart and shattered the rocks. Then came an earthquake (probably to shake some sense into Elijah). Then fire—if that wasn't enough. After all that, God showed up, speaking in a gentle whisper (1 Kings 19:11-13).

Elijah *still* pouted.

"I have been very zealous for the LORD God Almighty," he said. "The Israelites have rejected your covenant, torn down your altars, and put your prophets to death with the sword. I am the only one left, and now they are trying to kill me too" (1 Kings 19:14).

Reliance on God

Like Elijah, you need God's help to let go. Maybe you've believed the lies that nothing will ever change and you'll never be able to forgive. And where did those lies comes from? Satan. John 8:44 tells us the enemy of God "was a murderer from the beginning. He has always hated the truth, because there is no truth in him. When he lies, it is consistent with his character; for he is a liar and the father of lies."

Today, instead of believing the lie, choose the truth. It's in there somewhere and it all starts in the mind. When we are hindered in our prayer life or have no desire to read the Bible we are actually under *attack*. Don't allow your fears to breed. Rely on God.

After Elijah challenged God, he was told that there were, in fact, seven thousand people who had not bowed down to Baal. Elijah had believed he was all alone, but all the time he was standing with a great spiritual army! Satan is a liar. Have the courage to call it like it is.

Whatever false belief causes you to stumble can be tracked back to two sources: Satan, the father of lies, or *you*—when you choose to believe the lies. Fear likes to walk away with our thoughts. "I can't make it," we say. "God doesn't love me." "I'm not good/smart/pretty/skinny enough." "I don't deserve to live." "I'll never make it!" These are lies. All lies.

Fear can breed a reliance on God. Knowing we have something that we can't understand, control, or want, can be the groundwork of epic faith. —Daniel, 24

The enemy's job is almost too easy. He knows once we act upon the lie it becomes a sin. That's why it's important to renew the mind. That's the first step toward forgiveness. The only way to truly worship God is to give our body, our mind, and our fears as a living and holy sacrifice.

> Therefore, I urge you, brothers and sisters, in view of God's mercy, to offer your bodies as a living sacrifice, holy and pleasing to God—this is your true and proper worship.

Do not conform to the pattern of this world, but be transformed by the renewing of your mind. Then you will be able to test and approve what God's will is—his good, pleasing and perfect will (Romans 12:1-2).

I feel like the battle is all in the mind. Satan gets to us when we are vulnerable and broken, when our mind is easy to penetrate. He plants ideas in there that don't line up with the word of God. You are to overpower these thoughts and focus on God's Word. The more you meditate on the Word of God, the harder it is for Satan to plant those thoughts and ideas. —Alisha, 30

When we allow God to change the way we think we combat the lies of Satan. We can take our thoughts captive by praying Scripture over each individual lie. This can sometimes feel like it takes all day. Too many lies, not enough time. But there is good news. Once the fog lifts and our minds clear, we learn and know what God's will is for our lives. His good and pleasing and perfect will.

We don't have to cower in a spirit of fear. Instead, we can learn through the power of the Holy Spirit to discipline our minds and accept God's love. That love is stronger than any situation we find ourselves in. Knowing this, we can throw off the lies that kept us back!

Therefore, since we are surrounded by such a great cloud of witnesses, let us throw off everything that hinders and the sin that so easily entangles. And let us run with perseverance the race marked out for us, fixing our eyes on Jesus, the pioneer and perfecter of faith (Hebrews 12:1-2).

Don't let the lies grab and pull you down any longer. I'd like to share with you a powerful and transformative prayer by Neil T. Anderson. Pray it with me now:

We know that You are always here and present in our lives. You are the only all-knowing, all-powerful, ever-present

God. We desperately need You, because without Jesus we can do nothing. We believe the Bible because it tells us what is really true. We refuse to believe the lies of Satan. We stand in the truth that all authority in heaven and on earth has been given to the resurrected Christ. Because we are in Christ, we share His authority in order to make followers of Jesus and set captives free. We ask You to protect our minds, and lead us into all truth. We choose to submit to the Holy Spirit. Please reveal to our minds everything that You want to deal with today. We ask for and trust in Your wisdom. We pray for Your complete protection over us. In Jesus' name.[1]

Comfortable in Suffering

I wonder how our perspective would change if we viewed the spiritual battle as a literal war…*because it is.* I've never felt comfortable with the idea of war…even though I lived next to a military base for more than twenty years. The signs that say *Complacency Kills, Dangerous, Stay Out, Restricted Access,* or *Authorized Personnel Only* leave me feeling *un*comfortable. I know I'm protected, but I'm not the one fighting on the front lines. My ears are conditioned to bombs going off, windows rattling, and the house shaking at all hours of the day and night. It's no wonder that I don't even hear the banging, popping, and rattling anymore.

When it comes to our own emotional, spiritual, and sometimes physical battles, we're easily intimidated. The spiritual battle is always personal, but the Bible says we have everything we need. So why do we hide?

> Praise be to the God and Father of our Lord Jesus Christ, who has blessed us in the heavenly realms with every spiritual blessing in Christ (Ephesians 1:3).

Maybe the problem is that we don't feel prepared. How can you feel like you have everything you need for the fight when you know it's going to be a sneak attack? One moment you're fine and the next minute...*boom.* You're broken again. After many victories in Christ, we really should know better, right?

We should know better, but we don't. It seems that no amount of prayer or taking thoughts captive will help you overcome. But did you know that the Bible says that no weapon forged against you will prevail (Isaiah 54:17)? The outcome is always the same. Jesus is always victorious.

> We are more than conquerors through him who loved us (Romans 8:37).

We can be confident that in the spiritual battle we have everything we need. No matter how personal the battle becomes, we can be fully convinced that "neither death nor life, neither angels nor demons, neither the present nor the future, nor any powers, neither height nor depth, nor anything else in all creation, will be able to separate us from the love of God that is in Christ Jesus our Lord" (Romans 8:38-39).

Remember Shadrach, Meshach, and Abednego? They had the right perspective. They knew that even if God chose *not* to save them they would be quickly ushered into His literal presence. They weren't afraid anymore.

Today, choose to be thankful. The Lord always hears your cries. Ask Him to lead you to the towering rock of safety—Him. He is your safe refuge, a fortress where your enemies cannot reach you. Ask God to let you live forever in His sanctuary, safe beneath the shelter of His wings!

Welcome to the Spiritual Battle!

I know the word *welcome* sounds more like it should be on a doormat. Whoever heard of someone welcoming you into the spiritual battle—like it's a good thing? The fact is, we are at war against sin. The spiritual battle is real. Do you want to give yourself an advantage over sin? Fight it. And keep fighting. Billy Graham said, "If only we would begin at the *root* of our problems, which is the disease of human nature that the Bible calls sin!"[2] In his devotional *Unto the Hills* he encourages believers to fight sin...and not each other. How powerful is that?

Maybe you're having a hard time forgiving someone who calls themselves a Christian.

Maybe you're prone to gossip and your way of feeling better about yourself is to get even by smearing their name in the mud.

> You will be accepted if you do what is right. But if you refuse to do what is right, then watch out! Sin is crouching at the door, eager to control you. But you must subdue it and be its master (Genesis 4:7 NLT).

God does not fear evil, and neither should we. God challenges evil to show itself fully, so that in its defeat He might be all the more glorified. God gets glory through our weakness—which we will discuss further later in this chapter. Whatever the wicked imagine against us will come to nothing, because God's hand is greater, and He shall prevail. Evil will come. It will afflict us and those whom we love, but we have no reason to fear it or cower from it, because the victory is already complete. Pain can only bring us closer to the heart of God and bring more glory to the throne of Him who crushed it under His foot on the cross.

What happens if you can't crush sin in your life? How do you master sin? I challenge you to take up and put on the armor of God daily. Ephesians 6:11-17 says,

> Put on the full armor of God, so that you can take your stand against the devil's schemes. For our struggle is not against flesh and blood, but against the rulers, against the authorities, against the powers of this dark world and against the spiritual forces of evil in the heavenly realms. Therefore put on the full armor of God, so that when the day of evil comes, you may be able to stand your ground, and after you have done everything, to stand. Stand firm then, with the belt of truth buckled around your waist, with the breastplate of righteousness in place, and with your feet fitted with the readiness that comes from the gospel of peace. In addition to all this, take up the shield of faith, with which you can extinguish all the flaming arrows of the evil one. Take the helmet of salvation and the sword of the Spirit, which is the word of God.

Why put on the armor of God? Because it helps you…

- Live in the world, but not of the world
- Demolish strongholds in your life
- Get rid of everything that sets itself up against God
- Make your thoughts and fears obedient to Christ
- Go on the offense

The idea of taking "every thought captive" can take a while to grasp. It took me a whole year to feel like I was starting to be able to do it, and it felt like the battle over sin would never end. It can be so easy to constantly struggle with fear. We can become afraid to fight against the enemy. We're too afraid to strike back!

This reminds me of a story found in 2 Kings 13. The prophet Elisha asked King Jehoash of Israel to strike the ground with a bow and arrow. Once—twice—three times the king obeyed. Elisha was angry and said, "You should have struck the ground five or six times; then you would have defeated Aram and completely destroyed it. But now you will defeat it only three times" (2 Kings 13:19).

Have you ever felt you don't have enough strength to fight? Against past hurts? Future fears? Present circumstances?

It's not a choice.

You.

Must.

Fight.

HARD.

But don't worry. God's got you covered.

> The LORD is my strength and my shield;
> my heart trusts in him, and he helps me.
> My heart leaps for joy,
> and with my song I praise him (Psalm 28:7).

Today, ask the Lord to help you be strong in Him and in His mighty power. Take time to familiarize yourself with the armor of God and what each piece is used for. Take extra time in prayer and mentally "put on" all of the pieces of armor listed below. Ask God for strength for the day-to-day battle against the evil rulers and authorities of the unseen world. Finally, thank Jesus for the victory that already belongs to you.

- The Belt of Truth (Ephesians 6:14)
- The Breastplate of Righteousness (Ephesians 6:14)
- The Shoes of the Gospel of Peace (Ephesians 6:15)
- The Shield of Faith (Ephesians 6:16)
- The Helmet of Salvation (Ephesians 6:17)
- The Sword of the Spirit—the Word of God (Ephesians 6:17)

Boast About What?

You might be familiar with the verse that says we can boast about our pain. This comes right after Paul talks about having begged God to take away his constant fleshly weakness.

> So now I am glad to boast about my weaknesses, so that the power of Christ can work through me. That's why I take pleasure in my weaknesses, and in the insults, hardships, persecutions, and troubles that I suffer for Christ. For when I am weak, then I am strong (2 Corinthians 12:9-10 NLT).

Paul dealt with a struggle that he called his "thorn in my flesh." Three separate times he asked God to take it away from him, but each time God responded with, "My grace is sufficient for you." You might read that as a slap in the face to Paul, but surprisingly it wasn't. In the same verse, Paul was able to say that he boasts and even takes pleasure in his weakness.

Say what?

Honestly, it's too easy to gloss over this verse like hearing a Sunday school story for the thousandth time. Or like viewing a flannel graph that only highlights the good parts. But when was the last time you rejoiced—or even bragged—about your shortcomings? Your fatal flaws? Your constant fleshly weakness?

Seriously. I know what you're thinking.

We're pretty good at figuring out our strengths. And we're even better at bragging about them. You might have taken Myers-Briggs®, Strengths Finder 2.0, Strengths Deployment Inventory, or the Four Temperaments Test.

My parents taught me early on how to be a leader. They made sure I read many books on leadership. I remember feeling embarrassed the first time I truly felt weak. I liked picturing myself as strong. It's not that principles of leadership and wisdom are bad, per se, but sometimes I missed the chance to let God's power shine through my weakness and inability. God tells us, that if we want to be first in His kingdom, we have to become last on this earth. He tell us that His grace is enough for us.

Get it now?

It's not that Paul wants us to brag about our weakness, but the fact that God has our back. He is enough, remember?

> Think about it: Just as a parent disciplines a child, the LORD your God disciplines you for your own good (Deuteronomy 8:5 NLT).

Today, may we accept the challenge of learning how to boast about our weaknesses instead of in our own strength. It's not about how quickly we can perform a task, but how quickly we obey along the way. When you are afraid you can put your trust in God. Praise Him for the promise of a future and a hope.

Isn't it amazing that when faced with the choice to trust in God, we sometimes choose to be afraid of what man can do?

In all the stories that came out of that shooting in Colorado, one was truly a miracle. One of the victims, Petra Anderson, was hit by a bullet which struck her nose and traveled into her brain. But she didn't die. Her pastor, Brad Strait, blogged about her miracle. He said,

> The doctor explains that Petra's brain has a small "fluid pocket" in it. It is a tiny route of fluid running through her skull like a tiny vein through marble, winding from front

to rear. Only a CAT scan would catch it, and Petra would have never noticed it…But what is significant is that in Petra's case, the shotgun buck shot, maybe even the size used for deer hunting, enters her brain from the exact point of this channel. The bullet is channeled from Petra's nose through her brain. It turns slightly, and comes to rest at the rear of her brain. And in the process, the bullet misses all the vital areas of the brain. In many ways, it almost misses the brain itself, doing very little damage. Like a giant BB through a straw created in Petra's brain before she was born it follows the perfect route. The bullet moves in the least harmful way. A millimeter in any direction and the channel is missed. The brain is destroyed. Evil wins a round. [3]

Pastor Brad goes on to say, "In Christianity we call it prevenient grace: God working ahead of time for a particular event in the future." His grace is enough. Who knows why God allowed Petra to be a light in such a dark night and not someone else?

In our weakness, all we can do is come to the foot of the cross and ask for understanding. Ask for forgiveness from anyone who has hurt you or those you care about.

You Are Loved

There was a time when I wasn't living the Christian life. Nothing was working for me. I was so grossly focused on the shame of my past that I wanted to die. I couldn't see God's love in the midst of my suffering. It took a pastor's prayer over me for me to hear and understand three simple words:

You are loved.

I remember wanting to vomit. Have you ever been so turned off from God's love because of your circumstances that you wanted to throw up? I have. Our trials can make us feel worthless. Panic attacks can wreak havoc for months when we don't forgive and move on. Even though God uses health issues, anxiety, or our thorn in the flesh—it can still kick us in the butt until we feel raw. A verse I cling to when

I start to feel afraid again is Psalm 139:23—"Search me, O God, and know my heart; test me and know my anxious thoughts" (NLT).

Maybe you just broke up with the person you thought you were going to spend the rest of your life with.

Maybe a boss promised you a promotion and then fired you instead (or let you go).

Who can forgive under those circumstances?

Forgiveness is personal. It can feel like you're ripping your own heart out of your chest. Even the thought of it can make you anxious—and if you're anything like me, anxiety is your spiritual barometer. It makes you ask questions...questions like, "Are you living the way you know you should?" "Can you stop blaming others even if it's not your fault?" "Are you doing to others as you would wish them to do to you? Are you *really?*"

Can you answer those questions truthfully—without the whisper of the Holy Spirit pointing out the facts you'd rather ignore? Solomon wrote, "Truthful words stand the test of time, but lies are soon exposed" (Proverbs 12:19 NLT).

The question you need to be asking yourself is, "What lie (or lies) am I currently believing?"

You see, the problem isn't with God or the person who hurt you. *It's you!* Ask God to expose each and every painful lie you've believed so you can confess your sins and be forgiven. God is love. He wants to set you free. He wants to help you control the only thing (well, *person,* really) who can change your circumstances—yourself.

Don't expect it to be an easy process. Exposing lies is painful and our heart can't always be trusted. As the prophet Jeremiah writes, "The heart is deceitful above all things and beyond cure. Who can understand it?" (Jeremiah 17:9).

No matter how painful or how ugly you feel for being exposed, or how mad you are at God for allowing your heart to break, know that there is healing. If you remember only two things from this chapter let it be these:

First, He disciplines those He loves.

- "My son, do not despise the LORD's discipline, and do not resent his rebuke, because the LORD disciplines those he loves, as a father the son he delights in" (Proverbs 3:11-12).

- "Whoever loves discipline loves knowledge, but whoever hates correction is stupid" (Proverbs 12:1).

- "Those whom I love I rebuke and discipline. So be earnest and repent" (Revelation 3:19).

Second, He only prunes the parts of us that don't bear fruit. In John 15:2 Jesus tells us that God "cuts off every branch in me that bears no fruit, while every branch that does bear fruit he prunes so that it will be even more fruitful."

Second Timothy 1:7 says, "the Spirit God gave us does not make us timid, but gives us power, love and self-discipline." What is your number-one fear? Write down a prayer to God below. Acknowledge your fear and ask Him for His help to overcome.

Romans 12:2 says, "Be transformed by the renewing of your mind. Then you will be able to test and approve what God's will is—his good, pleasing, and perfect will." What do you think God's will is for your life? Ask God to help you change the way you think about a tough situation in your life. Then thank Him for His good, pleasing, and perfect will.

Second Corinthians 11:30 says, "If I must boast, I will boast of the things that show my weakness." Do you feel you have every spiritual blessing you need in Christ? Are you currently lacking anything? What do you think Paul meant by boasting in his weakness?

Ephesians 6:11 says, "Put on the full armor of God, so that you can take your stand against the devil's schemes." Have you ever felt you don't have the strength to fight? Write down five or six things you can do today to fight HARD against the enemy!

Second Corinthians 12:9 says, "'My grace is sufficient for you, for my power is made perfect in weakness.' Therefore I will boast all the more gladly about my weaknesses, so that Christ's power may rest on me." Have you ever tried to boast about your weakness? What was the outcome? Have you ever been afraid of showing your weakness for fear that you might be fired, broken up with, or made fun of? What is one thing you can do today to ask God to help you change your current perspective and start boasting in your weakness instead?

Ephesians 2:4-5 says, "Because of his great love for us, God, who is rich in mercy, made us alive with Christ even when we were dead in transgressions—it is by grace you have been saved." Do you have God's love in your heart? Or is this something you'd say you're still working on?

CHAPTER 2

In the Name of Christ

Sometimes you need to give yourself permission to transition. Why? Because no one else can do it for you. There are things that only God can tell you...*if* you let Him.

> This is what the Sovereign LORD, the Holy One of Israel, says: "In repentance and rest is your salvation, in quietness and trust is your strength, but you would have none of it. You said, 'No, we will flee on horses.' Therefore you will flee! You said, 'We will ride off on swift horses.' Therefore your pursuers will be swift!" (Isaiah 30:15-16).

No one wants to admit his or her sin. Hypothetically, let's assume that you're in the clear—it was the other person who did *you* wrong. The hard part is waiting for this person to apologize. What if they never do? *Be careful.*

Your response to sin and unrighteousness might actually be clouded in selfishness and pride. Even so, your human emotions might feel justified. *Valid.* Oftentimes, if you think about it long enough you'll find your emotions are misleading. That's why God tells us to rest *in* repentance.

Even if you're the one hurt.

Even if you're the one fitting the broken pieces back together.

To give you time to heal. To give you time to let go of anger.

I love this verse from Psalms. It shows us what to do when we're not quite sure how to handle our anger: "Don't sin by letting anger control you. Think about it overnight and remain silent. Offer sacrifices in the right spirit, and trust the LORD" (Psalm 4:4 NLT).

Think about it. The Bible doesn't say, "Don't be angry." The psalmist seems to acknowledge that you're angry and warns you against letting those emotions control you.

Maybe someone has hurt you in more intimate ways than anyone else could. They broke your spirit. Destroyed your innocence. Stole your worth.

But that doesn't have to be the *end* of the story. Jesus gives us the choice to accept His Living Water so we'll never be thirsty again (John 4:14). God can put back, fill in, and complete the pieces of our lives that were broken by unforgiveness. He won't leave us hanging or abandon us in our anger. He can handle our fears. Hurts. And that's why He tells us not to flee—because He can handle our anger. Trust me—I *know* how hard it is to hear the word *remain*. You don't want to remain in Him—you want to fly off the handle!

One thing that keeps me from extending forgiveness to others including myself is the pace of life. It's too fast to ponder what needs to be resolved. —Rob, 29

What's the most difficult time of day for you? For me, it's the evening. That's usually when the stress of the day takes over. I *feel* everything. It makes it harder to distinguish between truth and emotion. That's when I hurt the most. It's easier to want to act on impulse. That's usually when we do the most damage. Yell at whoever hurts us. Say mean-spirited things we didn't intend. Write quick, frustrated messages to the person who's wronged us over social media instead of saying it in love—and in person.

I don't know about you, but my heart takes time to process emotions. It's okay to need time to think things through—especially a situation where you're not sure how to forgive. Pray about it. Ask God what He thinks so you don't sin. Ask Him if you are justified before making a move. If you can think of the person who wronged you without wanting to make them feel the same physical, emotional, or spiritual pain you feel, then you might be ready.

> For we know him who said, "It is mine to avenge; I will repay," and again, "The LORD will judge his people" (Hebrews 10:30).

> "If you are even angry with someone, you are subject to judgment! If you call someone an idiot, you are in danger of being brought before the court. And if you curse someone, you are in danger of the fires of hell" (Matthew 5:22 NLT).

Ouch. That reminds me of words that I've said or actions that I've done in anger. What about you? If you find yourself struggling to stay silent, give yourself enough time to own up to *your* side of things. Realize what *you've* done.

Yes, you!

Good Story, Bad Story

Good idea: giving a small child a balloon. Bad idea: giving a small child a bunch of balloons. Growing up, I used to watch a show called *Anamaniacs* on television. They had the cutest animation with fun furry animals, so of course I loved it! One of my favorite parts were the "Good Idea, Bad Idea" segments. Some of them were silly and others uproariously funny, but the concept always stuck with me.

Maybe it's because in real life we really only have two options: good or bad.

Maybe it's because in real life not every story ends with *good*.

I'll start with the good story. Before I was married I liked this guy—I'll call him John. We met at a church event for young adults. It was the summertime and it was my first chance at a beach bonfire. I loved the smell of wet and sticky ocean air, sunscreen, and ooey-gooey marshmallows. John and I clicked *instantly*. Every time I made a joke he laughed. By the end of the night he ended up sitting next to me. It turned out that he and I were going to be in the same small group, and I was excited to get to know him. I knew he felt the same way. We exchanged phone numbers and something told me to *wait*. Let him contact me first.

I didn't wait. I initiated pretty much everything. Before long we were hanging out and he came to my birthday party…with another girl.

I always journal and look at my study Bible or a verse book that has specific subjects in it. The really cool thing about God is He knows what you need. Sometimes you just have to let Him show you. —Emily, 21

I was shocked. When I talked to him about it, I discovered that in fact they were dating. I'd had no idea he wasn't single. In all the times we'd hung out he'd never once spoken about her. Looking back, I should have been deterred, but I didn't listen to that still, small voice.

I kept pursuing John.

I couldn't help but think his flirtatious advances toward me meant something. It wasn't long before we were back to hanging out a lot. When he broke it off with that girl I thought, *This is my chance!*

Wrong. I pulled aside one of my friends at church to tell her about John. Ask for her advice. She was the only one I told about him.

A few weeks later I find out they were dating.

To say I flew into a jealous rage was an understatement. I said things to both of them that I deeply regret. For the first time in my life I wasn't concerned about my Christian good-girl image. I didn't hide my feelings or the gaping wound in my heart. Although I am certainly *not* proud of the way I handled things, I am grateful that both John and my friend extended forgiveness to me.

They never meant to go behind my back. It just happened that they had a deeper connection. My friend went the extra mile, and without telling me, prayed God would bring my future husband—soon! Funny, I met my husband, Marc, a few months after this happened. God used a really awkward and hurtful situation to draw me closer to Him and teach me how to forgive.

I'll end with the bad story. A friend and I had argued, and I tried everything to reconcile the situation. I called her, bought a dozen roses, showed up at her workplace, and spoke to our pastor.

Nothing I did worked.

In fact, it drove her further away from me. This girl and I were friends through church. She would come over to my apartment and would talk for hours about life. I met her when I was going through a rough patch personally. I so appreciated her friendship. It meant the world that she was there for me. One night at church I saw her and tried to talk to her—like I usually did. She was completely closed off to me, so I told her to send me a message later in the week when we could get together.

Instead she deleted me from Facebook. But that was before she sent me a nasty message about how I wasn't a Christian and God wouldn't bless the book I was about to publish, *Faithbook of Jesus*. I was exasperated.

I met with our pastor, tried contacting her, and did everything I could think of to resolve the situation. I surrendered. I tried to think of any reason why she would write such things about me. Instead of wanting to get together with me, she hid. A few weeks later she was let go from her position at church and moved halfway across the country

I was devastated. I felt that I had been robbed of our friendship. She never gave me the chance to apologize because she never told me what I did wrong. I decided to end our non-existent friendship. I couldn't force her to be a friend.

God highlighted a verse on forgiveness throughout the painful process. It was a verse I must have read a hundred times before, but it never clicked until I couldn't resolve my issue with her. Have you ever felt the same way? Sometimes, when life goes south, God uses Scripture to come alive truly for the first time. I just love this verse,

> If you are presenting a sacrifice at the altar in the Temple
> and you suddenly remember that someone has something
> against you, leave your sacrifice there at the altar. Go and
> be reconciled to that person. Then come and offer your sac-
> rifice to God (Matthew 5:23-24 NLT).

I always read this verse thinking it was the other person's responsibility to approach *me*. What I didn't realize was that when she had an
issue against me, it was *my* responsibility to go to her.

The major thing is to keep doing what I know to do right now. God will not show
me right now what I need to be doing five years from now, or one year from
now, or one month from now. It is a process, one step at a time. There are times,
though, when I simply have to put my head down and push forward, knowing
that God will go before me every step of the way, or offer me forgiveness if I
mess up. —Stephen, 23

I did my part and left her part up to God. It did sting when I felt
like I had done everything right and gave her more than one opportunity to tell me what I did wrong so I could apologize.

I believe God is saying to us in Matthew 5:23-24, "What are you
waiting for?"

Go! Try anyway. Pursue righteousness.

Keep Away

When we've done all we can to rest and wait on God and then go
and be reconciled, we still have one more thing to do. Get rid of dis-
traction and keep it away. As the apostle Peter tells us, "Be alert and of
sober mind. Your enemy the devil prowls around like a roaring lion
looking for someone to devour" (1 Peter 5:8).

Ask God to show you how to pursue righteousness and unfailing
love. It's not just a one-time thing—otherwise why would God call us
to forgive not one time, not seven times, but seventy times seven times?

Thankfully, we serve a God who enjoys helping us find and sustain life, righteousness, and honor. We can thank Him by seeking Him first.

> But seek first his kingdom and his righteousness, and all these things will be given to you as well (Matthew 6:33).

Here's an example of the importance of putting first things (the kingdom) first! This is something I've seen done at church and a few women's retreats. Get a jar, some rocks, and some sand. First, fill the jar with sand. Can you fit any rocks in there? Maybe you can shove a few on top. Now, pour out the sand. Fill the jar with rocks. Now, pour the sand in the jar.

When you put first things (the rocks/God's kingdom) first, there's plenty of room for the little things (the sand/distractions) to fill in the space around them. When we take the time to pursue the biggest things (God), the rest should fit into place. Don't be afraid to give it time though. This isn't an overnight adjustment.

Today, I challenge you to write out a list of distractions that keep you from putting God's kingdom first. Write them down, including any names of people who need to experience your forgiveness. Then ask God what you should do about it next.

Hello, My Name Is "Hypocrite"

Isn't it interesting that both stories of forgiveness I just mentioned (the good and the bad) concerned people I met at *church*? Maybe that's why there are so many books and articles written on why people love Jesus but hate His body—the church.

Let me explain.

Have you ever shown up to an event and been asked to fill out a nametag? Your name on display for all to see. As we grow older we learn to associate names—including our own—with labels. This goes as far back as kindergarten or the playground, calling each other names. Some nicknames are cute and others—well—aren't worth repeating!

Can you think of a time when you might have struggled with a sin over and over again? While you were struggling with this question, would you have used the label *Christian*? Maybe you saw your name as *Failure* instead. Or *Hypocrite. Fat. Nerd. Adulterer.* God could never love you because your sin was too great.

The good news is that "all have sinned and fall short of the glory of God" (Romans 3:23). We *all* fall short. All. Not some people or only some Christians—all.

Psalm 25:3 says, "No one who hopes in you will ever be put to shame." If we're honest, isn't it sometimes hard to abandon our search for labels, identity, and purpose in this world for a heavenly calling instead? We want the *here* and *now.* You feel that you need to trust in a physical, tangible person.

Maybe that's why some of us escape into relationships. You cross the physical line. Instead of being concerned with holiness, you question, how far is too far?

Your intentions start off good initially, but after a few hard knocks, you crawl into a more comfortable space.

Maybe it's in the arms of a stranger.

Maybe it's in that bottle of alcohol hidden in your room.

Maybe it's the magazine under your bed.

I'm tempted to picture angels and demons battling over my next action, but I know it's much more complicated than that. My spiritual battles are when it just doesn't feel worth it to be a Christian anymore, even though I know that's not true. Feelings are powerful. —Matthew, 27

You make Sunday into a day just for show. You go to church and put on your best Sunday face. Deep down you're *not* happy. You're not even sure church is the place for you anymore. All you see is fakeness, facades, and masks.

More hypocrites.

If only there was just one person who could penetrate through to your heart. Make you feel whole again. There is, and that person is *Jesus.* He is the author of our life. He's just waiting for us to come to Him so He can change the outcome.

I have had three serious, committed relationships, none of them sexually pure. I have had a very, very difficult time forgiving myself because I was so hypocritical, allowing others to believe I was a great role model while fooling around with boyfriends and going way past the purity limit. I'm afraid of committing to the wrong person because I know what I'm capable of, and I don't want to allow myself or a man to go down the road of pushing the limit of "How much is too much until God's not happy anymore?" —Natalie, 25

Newsflash: God can start what He finished in your life. You can trust Him to do that! He is the Alpha and Omega—the Beginning and the End. The First and the Last. Don't let anyone else but Jesus have authority to speak into your life. To call you names. The words we use to define ourselves matter.

> But now, this is what the LORD says—he who created you, Jacob, he who formed you, Israel: "Do not fear, for I have redeemed you; I have summoned you by name; you are mine" (Isaiah 43:1).

True Transformation

Do you remember the story of Saul in the New Testament? Of all people, he certainly needed redemption. A name change. He was going around taking names and persecuting Christians (Acts 9:1). God knew Saul wouldn't change on his own, so He intervened on his behalf. And it started from the labels Saul wore from birth.

> You know my pedigree: a legitimate birth, circumcised on the eighth day; an Israelite from the elite tribe of Benjamin; a strict and devout adherent to God's law; a fiery defender of the purity of my religion, even to the point of persecuting the church; a meticulous observer of everything set down in God's law Book (Philippians 3:5-6 MSG).

God intervened in Saul's life. I love how God stepped in and delivered Saul from labels. God gave him a new name—Paul. None of that "pedigree" stuff mattered anymore. Read the rest of the above passage with me:

> The very credentials these people are waving around as something special, I'm tearing up and throwing out with the trash—along with everything else I used to take credit for. And why? Because of Christ. Yes, all the things I once thought were so important are gone from my life. Compared to the high privilege of knowing Christ Jesus as my Master, firsthand, everything I once thought I had going for me is insignificant—dog dung. I've dumped it all in the trash so that I could embrace Christ and be embraced by him. I didn't want some petty, inferior brand of righteousness that comes from keeping a list of rules when I could get the robust kind that comes from trusting Christ— *God's* righteousness. I gave up all that inferior stuff so I could know Christ personally, experience his resurrection power, be a partner in his suffering, and go all the way with him to death itself (Philippians 3:7-10 MSG).

Paul got a taste of God and wanted more. Everything else was garbage, rubbish, nothing. It's interesting when non-Christians curse, they'll often use a name they don't believe in.

Christ.

Why not swear on Muhammad or Buddha? What makes the name of *Christ* so important?

To Paul?

To us?

In the Name of Christ

In Christ there is forgiveness for our sins and the gift of the Holy Spirit (Acts 2:38). In Him we are healed of our sickness (Acts 3:6). We give up our lives on this earth to spend eternity with Christ in heaven (Acts 15:26). Christianity is the only religion where the "prophet" died *and* rose again. Even the demons know this and shudder.

Some Jews who went around driving out evil spirits tried to invoke the name of the Lord Jesus over those who were demon-possessed. They would say, "In the name of the Jesus whom Paul preaches, I command you to come out." Seven sons of Sceva, a Jewish chief priest, were doing this. One day the evil spirit answered them, "Jesus I know, and Paul I know about, but who are you?" Then the man who had the evil spirit jumped on them and overpowered them all. He gave them such a beating that they ran out of the house naked and bleeding (Acts 18:13-16).

In the name of Christ there is intense *power*. It is no wonder people use the name of Christ.

Today, as you search your sins, ask Him to forgive you, and thank Him that you can call upon His name without fear. You can forgive—*in the name of Christ*. If you need help remembering, try memorizing this:

> **C**omfort: Believe it or not, God comforts us in our trials (2 Corinthians 1:2-7).
>
> **H**ope: It's easy to lose hope, but we have an anchor for our souls (Hebrews 6:19).
>
> **R**edemption: It is finished! We are forgiven by His blood (Ephesians 1:7).
>
> **I**nitiative: It's not up to us to be saved. It is by His grace alone (Ephesians 2:8-9).
>
> **S**poken for: The Holy Spirit helps us forgive when we can't (Romans 8:26-27).
>
> **T**rust: You can trust Him for every need. Follow Him today! (Philippians 4:19).

Tell Jesus that you believe in Him. Even if you doubt. Even if you struggle with forgiving over and over and over again. God stands in your room with His nail-pierced, outstretched hands. He is waiting to welcome you (just like He welcomed Thomas, His doubting apostle) and show you what to do next.

How Many Times?

> Then Peter came to [Jesus] and asked, "Lord, how often should I forgive someone who sins against me? Seven times?" "No, not seven times," Jesus replied, "but seventy times seven!" (Matthew 18:21-22 NLT).

Larry Osborne, one of my former pastors, says we should *stand up* to trials and *run away* from temptation. It's so easy to do the opposite. If we're honest with ourselves, we've all had times when we've chosen to run away from painful trials—like forgiving someone who needs it.

God is slowly teaching me what it means to forgive, what it means to make a mistake, and what it means to forgive "seventy times seven" times. We all need boundaries, but we also all need the grace that our Father longs to lavish on us, which is sometimes done through the very wounds that hurt us. —Carla, 35

Here's a number for you. Jesus left the ninety-nine in search of you (Matthew 18:12).

One.

Love came down. He forgave us. And He would have done it for just *you*. Why is it, then, that instead of basking in His insurmountable forgiveness, we hoard our meager treasures, hide, or *refuse* to forgive seventy times seven?

Forgiveness is not based on luck or feeling. It stems from the all-consuming, loving, and unending power of Jesus Christ. He forgave us for *all* time. Once and for all, He took our past, present, and future.

Technically speaking, Jesus didn't mean we are to forgive seventy times seven times—or 490 times. What happens if somebody hurts you 491 times? The number was meant to be abstract and so big that you stopped counting the other person's sins. Here is a great example of this,

> As [Jesus] was speaking, the teachers of religious law and the Pharisees brought a woman who had been caught in

the act of adultery. They put her in front of the crowd. "Teacher," they said to Jesus, "this woman was caught in the act of adultery. The law of Moses says to stone her. What do you say?" They were trying to trap him into saying something they could use against him, but Jesus stooped down and wrote in the dust with his finger. They kept demanding an answer, so he stood up again and said, "All right, but let the one who has never sinned throw the first stone!" Then he stooped down again and wrote in the dust. When the accusers heard this, they slipped away one by one, beginning with the oldest, until only Jesus was left in the middle of the crowd with the woman. Then Jesus stood up again and said to the woman, "Where are your accusers? Didn't even one of them condemn you?" "No, Lord," she said. And Jesus said, "Neither do I. Go and sin no more" (John 8:3-11 NLT).

God doesn't want us to keep track how many times others sin against us. Rather the numbers prove that forgiveness *counts*. Once God forgives, the slate is wiped clean. He removes our sins as far as the east is from the west (Psalm 103:12). This is just another illustration to help us see how amazing God's forgiveness is.

Maybe some of us aren't aware of our sin and how it affects others. We need others to help us *count* for eternity. That's what we're really living for—right?

My brothers and sisters, if one of you should wander from the truth and someone should bring that person back, remember this: Whoever turns a sinner from the error of their way will save them from death and cover over a multitude of sins (James 5:19-20).

Help a Brother or Sister Out

Ask God to show you the importance of your brother or sister. If you can lead at least one person back to Christ, they will share a forever home in eternity with you. Think about it. If you only willingly love and forgive people who love you back, how does that make you any different from a non-believer? Even people who aren't Christians can be kind to their friends. Our job is to be a Christlike example.

I realize this may not sound very appealing, especially if you are still hurting and not eager to forgive. Next time you're tempted to run away from the trials of forgiveness, remember how much Christ loved you and died for you.

> But I tell you, love your enemies and pray for those who persecute you (Matthew 5:44).

Press Pause

Do you have a confession to make? I do. I am not always the best at confessing my sins. Sometimes I wait. I hold on to my hurt just a little while longer.

Sometimes we're afraid. Other times we feel justified. Dietrich Bonhoeffer said, "It is more difficult to maintain a life that avoids real issues than one which faces them."[1] Our life gets messy when we don't pause, confess, and deal with our emotions right away.

> But if we confess our sins, he is faithful and just and will forgive us our sins and purify us from all unrighteousness (1 John 1:9).

Again, I can't help but think how much God tries to get our attention. He asks us once again, "What are you waiting for?"

Think of it this way. In music composers put rests between the notes. The rests are periods of silence that give the music rhythm and meter and prevent it from being a jumble of sounds. We should all be familiar with the chilling sound of *dun dun dun dun—rest—dun dun dun dun–rest*. The pauses bring the music to life. We can discern and then understand what we're listening to.

Forgiveness is just like a symphony. When we take the time to *pause* and make a confession, our life suddenly starts to make sense again. How can you discern God's voice if you don't stop and take the time to listen? How will you ever forgive if you don't take the first step of stopping to recognize your own brokenness?

I love how forgiveness allows the Christian to take time to pause, pray, and confess.

God desires this for us because He is the only one who can help us make sense of our shortcomings and failures. He is the master conductor. He knows what He is doing. *Don't be afraid.* Even if you feel like you've really blown it this time, don't take another step before giving God all the ingredients of your life. Watch how He mixes them all together for His glory.

Press pause.

Then start by saying, "God, I've got something to confess."

Isn't that wonderful? God also uses our confession with each other to add another dimension and build character. Even if you don't feel like it, ask God to help you press pause and immediately make a confession. Then thank God for making your life sweet again.

Matthew 5:23-24 says, "If you are offering your gift at the altar and there remember that your brother or sister has something against you, leave your gift there in front of the altar. First go and be reconciled to them; then come and offer your gift." Have you ever asked someone to forgive you even if you still felt hurt? How long did you wait and why?

IN THE NAME OF CHRIST

Acts 2:38 says, "Repent and be baptized, every one of you, in the name of Jesus Christ for the forgiveness of your sins. And you will receive the gift of the Holy Spirit." What does the name of Christ mean to you? Have you felt or seen the power behind it? Describe such a time.

In Matthew 18:21 Peter says, "Lord, how many times shall I forgive my brother or sister who sins against me? Up to seven times?" Have you ever kept track of forgiveness? Have you ever decided that someone had gone "too far" to be forgiven?

Luke 18:13 says, "The tax collector stood at a distance. He would not even look up to heaven, but beat his breast and said, 'God, have mercy on me, a sinner.'" How long do you wait before you confess a sin? Have you ever felt like you've sinned too much to ask for forgiveness?

Matthew 18:28 says, "When that servant went out, he found one of his fellow servants who owed him a hundred silver coins. He grabbed him and began to choke him. 'Pay back what you owe me!' he demanded." Have you ever felt like a hypocrite? Describe a time when you refused forgiveness to someone else, even though you'd been forgiven by God.

CHAPTER 3

When God Says No

Did you ever play the game "Red Light, Green Light" as a kid? I loved that game. My toes inched closer and closer over the line until someone shouted "Green Light!" Maybe it's because I enjoy the thrill of a chase. My whole life I have faced insurmountable sufferings, and yet Jesus has brought me through them all. I hope you find as much meaning in this chapter as I did living it. One of the hardest but most meaningful lessons I've learned in my life is what happens when God says no.

When I was in high school, I developed a terrible case of eczema. It took the skin off my feet and face. I ended up in the hospital, and the drugs they gave me over the period of three days put over one hundred pounds of weight on my body in only ten months. It took six years for my skin to heal. I also struggled with extreme anxiety through this entire process.

In college, the eczema returned with a fury and took the skin off my hands. I was living in Texas at the time and couldn't complete a discipleship training program—something I knew God had called me to. It was another three years before my skin was back to normal. I raged against God for allowing me to suffer like this—and I vividly remember asking God to forgive me for being so angry. My anxiety returned, and this time I took medication to help me through.

After nearly ten years of intense physical suffering, I finally felt like I had overcome. I quit my job to become a writer and received my second book contract. But then the contract fell through. My anxiety was already through the roof, and now I wasn't sure how I would pay my bills. I knew full well that God had called me to make this risky move, and I wondered if He knew what He was doing.

But God wasn't through with me. He'd imprinted a message on my heart—a call to encourage those who are broken by fear of forgiveness, thinking their past is too much to overcome, their present too dark, and their future…hopeless. God worked slowly but persistently to bring me to a place where I could share my story and find spiritual—not just physical—healing. It was a long, grueling process. I am here to show you that it's worth the wait—even when your faith fails you and God is nowhere in sight! It reminds me of the story of Abraham…

> Yet he did not waver through unbelief regarding the promise of God, but was strengthened in his faith and gave glory to God, being fully persuaded that God had power to do what he had promised. This is why "it was credited to him as righteousness" (Romans 4:20-22).

Faith Is Not Dead

Be encouraged, friend. In these difficult times you don't need to just *get* more faith. When you're walking through the valley of the shadow of death, it's hard to be told by a well-meaning friend that your problems would be solved if you'd just *believe* harder. As Dietrich Bonhoeffer put it, "The exercise of faith cannot depend on our ability to keep on believing, because this would mean that the harder one tries, the more faith one will have—and we know this does not work. Faith is always our response to the love and faithfulness of God."[1]

But what happens when God seems to be silent? When all you hear is *no*, *no*, and more *no*? It reminds me of the story of Job. Remember this one?

By all accounts, Job was blameless, righteous, feared God, and shunned evil. He was the best of the best. So when Satan looked for a person to tempt away from God, Job was the obvious choice. God allowed Satan to test Job, taking away everything that was precious to him—his health, his fortune, his friends...even his children.

Satan tries to pull Christians away from their relationship with God. That can take shape in many forms like overwhelming temptation, a literal fight to influence our day to day decisions and to cause us to become depressed or hopeless or apathetic. —Shawna, 24

Job's wife was ready to be done with it. She advised her husband to "curse God and die" (Job 2:9). Then, at least, their suffering would be over. But Job? He wasn't giving up on God. He simply said, "The LORD gave and the LORD has taken away; may the name of the LORD be praised" (Job 1:21).

Whether we like it or not, God sometimes withdraws His protection to *test* our faith. It isn't that God is silent—in fact, it's quite the opposite. Actually, He is rooting for us all along, all through the suffering and trials we face. With His strength defending us, He knows we have the power to stand.

Take some time to read through Job's story in the Bible. Do you notice what's going on at the very beginning? God's proud of Job, and He's not afraid to say it. *God likes to brag about those He loves.*

Satan needed God's permission before doing anything to Job. Satan needs God's permission before he harms you too. So before you or I lift our itchy trigger finger and place blame, we need to come to a place where our hearts can truly say, "Naked I came from my mother's womb, and naked I will depart. The LORD gave and the LORD has taken away; may the name of the LORD be praised" (Job 1:21).

When times get tough, it can be so tempting to curse your spouse, children, family, friends, boss, or neighbor. You know what's harder?

Accepting the responsibility and choosing to remain silent. During past trials, I've said and done things I *deeply* regret. I've slandered. I've gossiped. Even if I had initially been in the right, my response was sinful.

I was the one embarrassed.

The Bible tells us that throughout all his suffering and pain, Job "did not sin by blaming God" (Job 1:22 NLT). I doubt many of us could say the same for ourselves. It's never fun to watch God strip your life bare for all to see. In my suffering, I didn't understand why He chose to call me out for His testing. Why not someone who *deserved* those trials? Someone who was less obedient?

I didn't get it. I still had to learn the truth of Romans 8:28—"We know that in all things God works for the good of those who love him, who have been called according to his purpose." *All things*—even my suffering.

I have trust issues. I've given so much to others only to have it to be used as a weapon later, whether it's a parent or best friend. It's hard to give people the benefit of the doubt! I tend to look at my past hurts while trying to prevent them.
—Jerrod, 26

Knowledge Without Repentance

When someone hurts me, my first response is to lash out and do as much damage to her reputation as I can. But I'm learning to press pause and listen to the still, small voice of the Holy Spirit before I lose control. (Sometimes that still, small voice feels more like a punch to the face!) One thing I am still learning is to refuse to pass the blame until I've requested an audience of one. When you're most tempted to pick up the phone and text, call, post on social media, or email those closest to you, try dropping to your knees instead.

Have you ever lashed out about a person to someone who you knew would sympathize and agree with your side of the story? Friends and family are important, but oftentimes their advice—as we will see with Job's story—is dead wrong.

> After the LORD had said these things to Job, he said to Eliphaz the Temanite, "I am angry with you and your two friends, because you have not spoken the truth about me, as my servant Job has. So now take seven bulls and seven rams and go to my servant Job and sacrifice a burnt offering for yourselves. My servant Job will pray for you, and I will accept his prayer and not deal with you according to your folly. You have not spoken the truth about me, as my servant Job has." So Eliphaz the Temanite, Bildad the Shuhite and Zophar the Naamathite did what the LORD told them; and the LORD accepted Job's prayer (Job 42:7-9).

As Job's friends come to offer their support and encouragement, they offered all sorts of spiritual arguments for why Job was suffering. Maybe he'd sinned, and God was punishing him for his disobedience. Seems like a reasonable response to the situation…but God was extremely angry with Job's friends because they did not speak of Him as Job did. Wait, what?

How could they be so correct and yet be so wrong?

These men—Job's friends—had offered correct statements about God (yes, sometimes God *does* allow us to suffer as a result of our straying from His law), but none of them led Job to a place of *repentance* or a greater *acknowledgment* of God.

You can be entirely correct in your thoughts about God, but that doesn't mean you're not in danger of His anger and wrath.

God is altogether just and righteous, even when it may not always appear to be so! As the prophet Isaiah said so many centuries ago…

> "My thoughts are nothing like your thoughts," says the LORD. "And my ways are far beyond anything you could imagine. For just as the heavens are higher than the earth, so my ways are higher than your ways and my thoughts higher than your thoughts" (Isaiah 55:8-9 NLT).

God is the Creator, and we are the creation. We can't possibly comprehend everything He thinks or the way He's working in the world and in our lives. When Job cried out to God, demanding to understand why he was suffering so greatly, God responded, speaking to Job in a storm (or whirlwind as some translations have it). He said, "Who is this that obscures my plans with words without knowledge?" (Job 38:2). The Lord goes on to describe all the ways in which He is higher than Job—a mere mortal. The Lord made the earth and everything in it. Nothing happens that He doesn't control.

God still speaks out of storms today. When we most need to hear Him, He's there with an answer. As my husband says, "We need God out of a vortex. We need a God who devastates! We need a God who shatters our thoughts—even our correct ones. A God who communicates something that is more dear and more precious than correct statements about Himself but rather the knowledge of Himself as He is, in fact, awesome, holy, fearful, and to be dreaded. When you have words without knowledge, it means that they are correct but not knowledgeable."

Sounds like a paradox? It's not. C.S. Lewis says that "Nothing less will shake a man—or at any rate a man like me—out of his merely verbal thinking and his merely notional beliefs. He has to be knocked silly before he comes to his senses. Only torture will bring out the truth. Only under torture does he discover it himself."[2]

Job was described as "upright." He was an exemplary man. Yet however exemplary his condition was, he still had to go through the fire. God allowed the enemy to devastate his life by taking away everything that mattered to him. No matter how eloquent our words or the words of our friends to explain the human condition, they are *still* words without knowledge. My husband goes on to say, "We have not been demanded of enough. We're getting by with murder, casual hellos, cheap amens and hallelujahs, singing a few choruses while filling a bucket or collection plate and looking religious on Sunday. Only God knows your true condition as He sees it, not you. He knows the truth of your life, your marriage, your morality, your thoughts, your secret dealings; He knows you perfectly."

We have a lot of words without knowledge and a lot of raising our hands without true worship. I appreciate my husband for helping me to see the story of Job as I hadn't been challenged to see it before. When we demand an answer of God, it probably won't be the answer we expect.

And whether we get that answer in this life or the next is up to God. That's the hardest part.

I have to be aware that Satan has thousands of years of experience in destroying people. I have to rely on my God and not myself to defeat him. —Jennie, 30

Whether you take the worldly knowledge of a friend at face value or whether you seek to go deeper like the Bereans (Acts 17:11) and run everything by God is up to you! Do you want to know what Job said when he finally "got" it? He said,

> I know that you can do all things;
> no purpose of yours can be thwarted.
> You asked, "Who is this that obscures my plans without
>   knowledge?"
> Surely I spoke of things I did not understand,
> things too wonderful for me to know.
> You said, "Listen now, and I will speak;
> I will question you,
> and you shall answer me."
> My ears had heard of you
> but now my eyes have seen you (Job 42:1-5).

If you read Job's response closely, you will finally see where God has been "hiding" this entire time. God was already *in* the midst of so much devastation!

He *knew.*

He is *all*-powerful.

He is the same yesterday, today, and forever (Hebrews 13:8).

So when it seems like He's silent, remember that God is willingly choosing *not* to intervene. And in all of Job's afflictions, He was Himself afflicted. God was never some passive observer. Job asked the questions, as we ought to ask the questions.

God pretty much drags me screaming and kicking with no choice in the matter!
—Stephanie, 27

Like Job, God can handle your questions, your misinterpretations, and even your anger.

Why are You silent?

Why are You allowing it?

What am I supposed to understand from this?

We're suffering from an inadequate knowledge of God, and yet we are the Church. The house of God. The body of Christ.

We should know better.

We don't like to view God as someone who lets bad things happen to good people—like Job. Our society simply has no tolerance for suffering. God is here to show you in mighty, mighty ways that there is room for repentance.

In God's kingdom, forgiveness reigns.

Control Freak

Suppose you could see God right now, just as He is in all His glory. His holiness would cause you to fall on your knees in repentance. Would you fall down? Or would your control-freak nature start asking questions and demanding answers?

"*Why* didn't You stop me before I sinned?"

"*Why* couldn't You have healed me earlier? After all, You *are* God!"

It's questions like this that plague my mind and probably yours too. What is it about our control-freak nature that makes us try to reason with and figure out the nature of God? His characteristics? The reasons why He does what He does? It's insanity, I tell you...*insanity*!

The more you see God's hand in your life, the more you can't help but rejoice. God's faithfulness is never-ending. So why do you become resentful and discontented and give up? You know better, but when you suffer you're overwhelmed with bitterness, anger, fear, and resentment. You can't see straight. You yearn for more answers and come up short. The control freak in you and in me wages war against God. Faith wrestles with the enemy, and sometimes we lose. Fortunately for Job—and for us too—God *did* answer.

It takes a *real* man or woman of faith to question God. If that doesn't blow (literally) the lid off your control-freak nature, I don't know what will. Thankfully, we don't have to be afraid of God's response. Because of Jesus's work on the cross, we don't have to hide our questions! We can come boldly and confidently into God's presence. Today, ask God for His mercy and grace to approach Him.

Talk to Him.

Get comfortable in His presence, even when you start to question if God is really there. Remember Job.

I know better. I know what I should do and I've trusted God before. I get frustrated that I have to learn the same thing all over again. It's hard to have faith when I'm being a control freak. —Jennifer, 28

All Hope Is Not Lost

In the dark seasons, we feel lost and don't understand a thing. Maybe it's because we're not supposed to! We're supposed to cry and whine because God is making us into a new person. He is taking out our stony heart of sin while replacing it with a tender, responsive heart (Ezekiel 36:26). Sure, it takes time, but God is at work cleaning us up. Looking back on our control-freak natures and sheer resistance to God's will should make us cry.

How sinful are we to tell God what He can and cannot do in our lives?

God never tells you the reason for your suffering while you're going through it. That reason is only made clear on the other side of the struggle. If we didn't experience the trial, what would we ever learn? It reminds me of the story of Abraham.

When I couldn't find a steady job for over two years, I was really mad. I felt like I was doing all I could. I finally stopped worrying and prayed for God's will, no matter how long it took. Although the process wasn't easy, fun, or enjoyable, God provided. We made it. Now I have an awesome job with an awesome guy, and I was able to be home with my kids for some precious times. It was a huge win-win looking back. —Brock, 30

Abraham was a man of God. He was 75 years old when God called him and his wife, Sarah, to an unknown place. This would be their very own special place—a place of blessing. God said that everyone in the world would be blessed through Abraham, and that his descendants would be as numerous as the sand on the seashore. The only problem? Sarah couldn't get pregnant. They had no children.

Abraham's faith gained him God's favor. I love that Abraham knew how to tell God exactly what was on his mind. He said, "O Sovereign LORD, what good are all your blessings when I don't even have a son?" (Genesis 15:2 NLT).

The Lord reassured Abraham and promised him many children— as many as the stars in the sky. By this time, Abraham and Sarah were coming up on their one hundredth birthdays. Still no babies in sight. Sarah got impatient and told Abraham to sleep with her servant, Hagar. They decided to do it *their* way instead of waiting on God's blessing— which seemed to be taking longer than it was supposed to. Hagar gave birth to a son named Ishmael. God once again revealed more of Himself and called Abraham to believe. But instead of having faith, Abraham basically told off God, just about demanding that Ishmael "live under your special blessing" (Genesis 17:18 NLT).

Do you like to read between the lines? If you're like me, you'll see Abraham *tell* God how to bless him and his family. Digging a little deeper, we find what Abraham is *really* asking God to do is bless his sin. *This* is scary.

How often are we like Sarah? We can't wait.

How often are we like Abraham? We try to tell God what to do.

I think part of asking God to forgive your sin is being honest with God, like Abraham. He was never afraid to tell God his feelings. I remember when I was waiting on my future husband. My friend Angela told me to stop trying to *force* a relationship with Ishmael because God wanted to bless me with Isaac. No matter how many guys I tried to put into the role of my future husband, they weren't Marc.

I had to wait.

But let's not miss the point. God not only blessed Ishmael as Abraham requested, but a year later Sarah gave birth to Isaac—the son that God had promised. Today, *tell* God about your struggles. Don't try to hide past decisions. He already knows and is waiting to bless you—just like He blessed Abraham.

The idea of right and wrong as very black and white was ingrained in me as a child, and I was taught that if I loved Jesus, I would never choose wrong. Through I realize now that's not true, it's hard to release that pressure and to focus on the relationship, which is where we find hope and the freedom to live forgiven. —Brittany, 24

You're Wrong

How could a loving God let me go through such agony?

We feel like we've been wronged. We feel like God's out to get us. Like maybe He needs our forgiveness for having hurt us so badly. (After all, isn't He in charge of everything?)

But really, we don't need to forgive God. He doesn't need our forgiveness. It's us.

I was wrong.

Below is a prayer I wrote many years ago when God told me I needed to let go. To forgive *myself* for everything I've ever gone through. Every bad decision I've made. No matter if He chose to heal me in that moment or not, I knew it was my responsibility to ask Him to forgive me because He was always right. Pray this with me right now!

> Dear Jesus, I invite You to come move in me. From the top of my head to the tips of my toes. I want You to come and remove all my hurts and all my fears and all my sins. I give them to You. Please forgive me. Please forgive me. Please forgive me. Please forgive me, Lord! I know, Lord, that You allowed me to go through this darkened dungeon so that one day I could come into the light and experience new life. Help me walk with You. Keep my feet from slipping. Let my life be beautiful. Teach me how to reach out to others and tell them about You, Jesus. That You died for us. That You save! That You can erase all the wrongs in our life and help us to overcome. Reconcile us, Jesus. I believe. Amen.

Remember, at the end of Job's life he got the redemption he was seeking. God finally answered him. All Job could do was to take back everything he said and be silent. He repented (Job 42:6). He admitted he was wrong.

> This is how we know that we belong to the truth and how we set our hearts at rest in his presence: If our hearts condemn us, we know that God is greater than our hearts, and he knows everything (1 John 3:19-20).

When All Else Fails, Pray!

Sometimes you give God your fears and ask for release from suffering...and He still says no. *How could a God who loves me continue to reject my desperate pleas for help?* you wonder. Now is the time to process your questions with a professional counselor, trusted relative, or a church elder or pastor. Surround yourself with wise people—not friends like Job's.

Is anyone among you in trouble? Let them pray. Is anyone happy? Let them sing songs of praise. Is anyone among you sick? Let them call the elders of the church to pray over them and anoint them with oil in the name of the Lord. And the prayer offered in faith will make the sick person well; the Lord will raise them up. If they have sinned, they will be forgiven. Therefore confess your sins to each other and pray for each other so that you may be healed. The prayer of a righteous person is powerful and effective (James 5:13-16).

When your prayers feel like they fall on deaf ears and you're tired of feeling like you're alone in your struggle, get help. That's when we need to pray, "I do believe; help me overcome my unbelief!" (Mark 9:24).

The God we worship today is the same God who came down to Earth to save us—the same God we read about in the Bible. He is still in the business of miracles. Let go of all your worries and concerns about the future. Don't allow unbelief to kill you any longer. Allow God to wash you clean in the forgiveness of His blood. By His stripes you are healed.

Even when you feel so humiliated in life.

Even when you're not so sure you feel like being honest with God.

Say it. Yes, I lost my joy. Yes, I feel like God slapped me in the face. Like He threw a bucket of cold water on me.

The problem may be too big, too right-in-front-of-you for you to see past. Maybe all you can see is a mean and angry God staring back at you. But remember: Just because God says no today doesn't mean He's saying not ever. Don't ever forget that.

Arise

Balloons are fun. They float for everyone to see. They look so peaceful in the sky. Have you ever see a little child holding on to a balloon? She or he looks up and admires it. It fascinates them. That is what the Lord wants us to be. *Fascinated.* Once we take hold of His hand, we're able to look up to and admire Him and His work in our lives. When we're burdened by past failures our future may not look too bright. Let's admire those who have gone before us.

Today, take some time to read Hebrews 11, also known as the "Hall of Faith" chapter. This passage is full of stories of people who made mistakes, screwed up, and got lots of things wrong, but accomplished great things for God because of their faithfulness.

Strive to be someone who is faithful even in the midst of failure. As Abraham Lincoln said, "I am not concerned that you have fallen. I am concerned that you arise."

Job 30:27 says, "The churning inside me never stops; days of suffering confront me." What is the toughest question you've ever asked God to answer? Did He respond? If so, how?

Take some time to read **Job 38–41**—God's response to Job's suffering. How is this an answer to Job's question? What does this teach you about God's nature?

Acts 9 tells the story of Paul's conversion. Verses 3-4 say, "As he neared Damascus on his journey, suddenly a light from heaven flashed around him. He fell to the ground and heard a voice say to him, 'Saul, Saul, why do you persecute me?'" Has God ever interrupted your life to give you hope in a way you never expected?

Psalm 51:4 says, "Against you, you only, have I sinned and done what is evil in your sight; so you are right in your verdict and justified when you judge." Do you struggle with choices you've made in the past? Why or why not?

Isaiah 45:24 says, "In the LORD alone are deliverance and strength. All who have raged against him will come to him." Describe a time when you felt angry with God.

Psalm 17:6 says, "I call on you, my God, for you will answer me; turn your ear to me and hear my prayer." Describe a time when you felt that God was speaking to you.

Mark 9:24 says, "I do believe; help me overcome my unbelief!" Have you ever struggled with unbelief in God? Was there ever a time when you felt like you couldn't believe?

Psalm 23:4 says, "Even though I walk through the darkest valley, I will fear no evil, for you are with me; your rod and your staff, they comfort me." What is the greatest challenge you are currently facing? Write out a prayer asking God to help you and be with you through this trial.

Lamentations 3:22-24 says, "Because of the Lord's great love we are not consumed, for his compassions never fail. They are new every morning; great is your faithfulness. I say to myself, 'The Lord is my portion; therefore I will wait for him.'" What is your greatest fear for the future?

PART 2

RESTORED

See, I am doing a new thing!
Now it springs up; do you not perceive it?
I am making a way in the desert
and streams in the wasteland.

ISAIAH 43:19

Chapter 4

A Good Place to Start

Have you ever read the story of Jonah? It's a short story that includes a whale. If you grew up in Sunday school like me, you mostly remember the whale part: Although it only has four chapters, there's enough angst in it to cover the entire Bible. From what little information we have, we know Jonah resents God's *big* heart and His love for people. The people of the city of Nineveh were falling away from God's will, and God commanded Jonah to go prophesy to them and help them repent of their wickedness.

But Jonah doesn't feel like it. So he runs and hides in a ship going not to Nineveh, but far away in the opposite direction.

Have you been there?

Like Jonah, we sometimes leave difficult situations too quickly. We know God has already forgiven this person, and we just don't have the heart to let them off the hook...*yet*. Maybe we want them to suffer for their sins a little bit more.

I find it interesting that a giant whale captured Jonah and forced him to stomach the situation. Literally. After three days, Jonah gave up (what else could he do?), and God made the fish spit him up. Jonah lived. You'd think Jonah would be happy at this point, but he wasn't. His pride still intact, Jonah went and preached the message to the *wicked* people of Nineveh. You can tell by his eight-word sermon Jonah was *not* impressed. He simply said, "Forty more days and Nineveh will be overthrown" (Jonah 3:4). His heart was *still* hardened; he clearly didn't want to be there. Jonah probably thought he'd get away with the shortest sermon in the Bible, but his plan backfired. The people *repented.* The people in this giant city took an entire three days to fast and show their sorrow outwardly. They didn't just say they were sorry— they lived it. Because of their change of heart, God took pity on them and saved the city from His judgment.

Before I continue bagging on Jonah, I want us to see how closely related we are. Have you ever met the family of a good friend and thought, *Wow, they're all just the same!* Yep, that's us. We're *just* like Jonah. If someone hurts us, we no longer want to associate with that person. It's hard to—even though we know deep down that God and others can so easily forgive them. Just like Jonah, we take personal offense when someone is forgiven.

I am in a difficult season of life right now. It seems nothing is going as I have planned for it to go, but I am being reminded to let go of my plans and not be so hard on myself and accept His forgiveness and freedom. At times it has been difficult to have hope. However, I find comfort in His Word and believe that no matter what the circumstances may be, one can always find hope and freedom in Christ. —Amelia, 26

If you were to make a list right now of people who've offended you, who would be on it? And going a step further, which eight words (like Jonah) would you use to tell them how badly he or she hurt you?

Every time I've been hurt, I've known in my heart that God forgave him or her, but I just didn't want to see it. Jonah didn't either.

He built himself a shelter and waited for God to burn down the city. When God relented and forgave the city, Jonah got angry enough to the point of death. *That was it for Jonah.* Because God forgave his worst enemy, life was no longer worth living. *Wow.* How sad is that? I hope you're not like Jonah! He held on to bitterness instead of rejoicing in the forgiveness he himself had been given.

Something happened in my childhood that caused a great deal of pain and grief from close family members. They've never apologized or recognized the wrong. I have faith in the Lord because I feel like He has freed me from a lot of that, but when it comes to dealing with those certain relationships, because of continual and ongoing pain, betrayal, and distrust, it is hard to have faith in people.
—Kristen, 24

Torn into Pieces

Let's say you decide to take your eight words to the person who wronged you. Would you start by taking it to God? Or would you use them to confront the person and rip him or her a new one? (Because let's be honest…he or she may deserve it.) Before you get mad or throw the book against the wall, hear me out. *Please!* The passage below is one of my all-time favorite Bible verses.

> Come, let us return to the LORD. He has torn us to pieces;
> now he will heal us. He has injured us; now he will bandage our wounds (Hosea 6:1 NLT).

I want to share a secret with you. I love this verse *because* it gave me permission to share those eight words. Sometimes I feel like my story of forgiveness is slightly unique, or maybe it isn't. The person I struggled with forgiving was me, myself, and I.

No matter what choices I made, my health worsened. I felt like my life was over. I was afraid that God would tear me to pieces and forget to bandage my wounds. My condition puzzled the doctors. My parents were scared. I was *disgusted*. But when my mom read those words from Hosea to me in the hospital, I was hooked. *Wait*, I thought. *There's a verse for my condition? I've never heard of anyone else losing his or her skin. Did God put that verse in the Bible specifically for me?*

That's when I knew I seriously needed to study the Word—on my own! Not just what I was taught in Sunday school. Not just during family devotions. I wanted God to speak to *me*.

Have *you* ever felt that way? You think you're the only one going through a specific problem and then you happen to find a verse that seems to be directly from God Himself?

I love that God is still in the business of speaking to us through the Word. This should bring you comfort while you are waiting for God to pick up the broken pieces of your life. As Kay Arthur puts it in her book *Lord, Heal My Hurts*, "Physical wounds infected or filled with debris will never heal properly. The wound must be discovered, opened, derided, and cleansed thoroughly. Then healing can come."[1]

I believe God tears us to pieces *so that* He can heal us. Friends, don't be afraid of Jesus's strong hands. Maybe God is allowing this person, event, or struggle in your own life to shape your character. I don't know about you, but I struggle with wanting to fix things fast. Forget about character—I just want to be well. Even when I see a friend hurting, I want to help him or her get over it *immediately*. Sometimes we can't. We *have* to let God do His thing because it is in the trial that God forges a new path and creates stronger character.

I don't have a hard time forgiving other people for some reason. But I do have a hard time forgiving myself. I haven't really figured that out yet...—Anne, 25

For I am about to do something new. See, I have already begun! Do you not see it? I will make a pathway through the wilderness. I will create rivers in the dry wasteland (Isaiah 43:19 NLT).

Something New

Life is a journey. I can say this with full confidence now. The first time I attended the San Diego Christian Writer's Guild I remember listening to Jerry B. Jenkins, the coauthor of the Left Behind series. He made Christian fiction famous. I was nineteen at the time with newly healed skin and a fresh heart to share God's truth. I hungered to be seen. Heard. *And read.* It took many years of obscurity to bring me to this place as a published author. I write to you as a broken individual who is full of God's grace and hope. I am a walking miracle trying each day to walk in the Spirit. Each day I pray—and I hope you'll pray with me—"I am ready for God to do a new thing."

When I was overwhelmed with pain and loneliness I used to run to cutting, to an affair, to despair. NOW I process by running to Jesus. Literally. I find a beautiful place to run to and stay in His presence until He gives me strength and grace to go on. —Julie, 39

One of the verses God uses to encourage us through tough transitions is Isaiah 43:19 (above). Each time you read that verse you can know for certain that God is preparing the way. No one ever wants to be the receiver of bad news. No one likes to suffer. No one. And yet God allows us to suffer anyway. Why? So we can rejoice. It sounds like something twisted, *but it's not.*

> We also glory in our sufferings, because we know that suffering produces perseverance; perseverance, character; and character, hope (Romans 5:3-4).

When was the last time you forgave someone? I'm guessing it was *because* of something bad that happened to you. God knows. Don't be afraid. Every day, God is in the process of doing something new, and if we're too concerned with past failures, present circumstances, or future fears we'll miss out. Life is a journey, suffering matters, and God will see you through.

The Real Question

I'm reminded of the story of Jesus and Peter. Jesus loved Peter very much, despite his rash decision-making, impetuousness, and crazy-talking mouth.

> Then Peter remembered the word Jesus had spoken: "Before the rooster crows, you will disown me three times." And he went outside and wept bitterly (Matthew 26:75).

Sometimes you make wrong choices knowing full well what you're doing—and what the consequences are likely to be. Like Peter, you just *can't stop*. You whine, complain, curse, or yell at others while deep down you're a wreck. Emotionally you're all over the place. Nothing makes sense.

I was going through a tough time. Depression and pressure kicked in. Nothing helped until God led me to 1 Peter 5:7. I sensed a huge weight lifted from my shoulders, knowing God cares for me and the smallest details in my life.
—Martin, 27

Maybe you're the one wrestling with choices from the past. You're in deep sorrow. You're not sure what to do or how to even begin to live again. Maybe you're bitter. The past didn't treat you well and you're wondering how to get even with those who caused you to suffer. No matter what the pain of the past, *God offers His hand.*

Before His crucifixion, Jesus warned Peter that he would one day deny Him. Peter was horrified at the idea. "No way!" he said. "I'll never deny You."

…But then he did. He denied that he had ever known Jesus…*three times.*

Ouch. Never make a deal you can't keep. Peter broke his word even after God gave him a warning. How do you make sense of that?

But the story's not over. I love what happens later. After Jesus had risen from the dead He was eating and chilling with His disciples. He took Peter aside during breakfast and asked him a tough question. He said, "Do you love Me?" (You can read the whole story in John 21:15-19).

Now, unfortunately we only have one word for love in the English language. In Greek there are *three* words. The first is *eros,* which means romance or sexual love. The second, *phileo* means a brotherly love. It suggests deep affection, like you have for your closest friends. *Agape* love is the strongest of all. It can't be earned but can only be freely given. It's a love that comes without expectations. This is the kind of love Christ showed for us when He died on the cross.

When Jesus asked Peter if he loved Him, He was talking about *agape*—the granddaddy of all love. Peter says, "Yes, Lord. You know that I love you." Sounds pretty good and nice...but they're not talking about the same thing. Jesus is asking, "Do you *agape* me?"

And Peter responds, "I *phileo* you." He's basically saying, "I heart you, friend."

That's not what Jesus wants. It's only *phileo* love. Jesus asks Peter again, "Do you *agape* me?"

"I *phileo* you," says Peter.

Jesus asks one more time. But this time he changes it up. "Peter, do you *phileo* me?" He says. "Do you heart me, friend?"

And Peter says, *"Yes!"*

I love how God knows how much we fail and screw up miserably. And yet He sees us in our pain and meets us where we are. He wants and tries for the best in each one of us. He knows us personally enough to know when we're not giving our all, or when we're not even capable of loving. What a fantastic day of questions for Peter and Jesus. I'm sure they both went away thinking, *Phew! That's a good place to start!*

Questions, Questions, and More Questions

Next time you're tempted to believe that God doesn't have your best interest at heart, ask Him the one question He asks Peter: "Do You love me?"

I'll never forget the time I was passing out hot chocolate at the Oceanside Pier with my friends from church. Instead of serving God in huge ways, we thought it would be a good idea to simply give people a warm cup of cocoa while telling them three words: *Jesus loves you.*

Funny, I wasn't expecting to be the one *offended.*

I grew up in the church and accepted Jesus into my heart when I was five years old. These words were nothing new to me—and yet they made me feel like I was standing on a soapbox preaching with a megaphone, screaming to those who walked by. I guess I thought sharing your faith should happen naturally with those you come into contact with at work, the store, or neighborhood. I knew I wasn't *that* comfortable on the pier, but we weren't yelling or being crazy. We were only giving away a free drink on a cold night. So why was I so angry?

Maybe it's because deep down I didn't *believe* Jesus loved me.

Maybe it's because I was jealous of the faith my friends had.

You owe it to me, BFF, to have been my friend forever. You owe it to me, boyfriend, to have kept from taking my heart. You owe it to me, ex-fiancé, to have fought for our relationship. You owe it to me, friend, to have not died and left me. You owe it to me, body, to have not gotten sick. You owe it to me, siblings, to have been there for me. You owe it to me, parents, to have protected me. My heart said: You all owe me. —Lisa, 31

At the end of the day, I wasn't happy with the person God made me to be. If Jesus loved me, why did the feeling of dread hang over my head? I wanted to shake the feeling, but for some reason I couldn't. God's love felt more like a body bag full of dead weight. Somehow, I *still* couldn't fathom how on earth I could accept God's love when I felt like He owed me so much more.

There's a reason why God asks us to guard out hearts (Proverbs 4:23). Our heart determines the direction of life. If we're upset it might cause us to second-guess our decisions and head in a different direction.

Like Peter, you might feel permanently unworthy of God's love. This is impossible. Nothing can *ever* separate us from God's love.

> For I am convinced that neither death nor life, neither angels nor demons, neither the present nor the future, nor any powers, neither height nor depth, nor anything else in all creation, will be able to separate us from the love of God that is in Christ Jesus our Lord (Romans 8:38-39).

That's why God asks us to come to Him as children. Children aren't afraid to tell their parents how they really feel, when they're afraid, or when they just need a hug. I love this quote from Billy Graham:

> A child does not repeatedly ask his parents whether he will be taken to a doctor if he becomes ill or whether there will be another meal to eat (at least, not very often in our culture). The reason he does not ask such questions is that his parents have proven to him over and over again that they love him enough to take care of his needs. It is the same with God.[2]

All we can see is failure. All Jesus sees is His precious child. Every morning Jesus wants us to bring our requests to Him and ask, "What's next?"

But instead we ask questions like…

- "What if my worst fear comes true?"
- "What if I fail?"
- "What if I can't forgive?"
- "What if I can't make enough money to support myself?"
- "What if my relationship is over?"

Friends, I'm here to tell you that we're rich because of God. He loved *you* first, and that's *why* we can love, serve, and forgive with our whole heart, soul, mind, and strength. How can you care about others when you're still focused on your own injustices? Call on the Father! The longer you and I fight to surrender, the longer we push against the loving arms of the Lord. We must choose to embrace the tightrope of adventure *right now*. Trust Him when He says He is going to take care of your needs.

I'm proud to say that night at the pier was a wakeup call for me. I knew I needed to start asking the right questions, even if it meant exposing my fears. Even if it meant saying out loud that I doubted God ever loved me. I needed to know that I am accepted. I am secure. I am significant. As Neil T. Anderson puts it, "Understanding who God is and who you are in Christ are the two most important factors in determining your daily victory over sin and Satan. False beliefs about God, not understanding who you are as a child of God, and making Satan out to be as powerful and present as God are the greatest causes of spiritual defeat."[3]

I know this to be true because I've lived it. Do you know it too? Do you understand that in Christ you too are accepted, secure, and significant? I hope it doesn't take more suffering and trials for you to recognize these truths. Why is it that trials are sometimes the only way we can understand spiritual truths like these?

- You are God's child (John 1:12).

- You are also Christ's friend (John 15:15).

- You are His saint (Ephesians 1:1).

- You are found complete in Christ (Colossians 2:10).

- You are completely free from condemnation (Romans 8:1-2).

- You can't be separated from God's love (Romans 8:35).

- You have not been given a spirit of fear but of power, love, and a sound mind (2 Timothy 1:7).

- You are God's coworker (1 Corinthians 3:9).

- You can approach God with freedom and confidence (Ephesians 3:12).

Our unrighteousness didn't stop Jesus from loving us enough to die on the cross for our sin. Thank God because, as Nancy Leigh DeMoss says, "The good news of the gospel is that the Great Physician has made available a cure for our deceived, diseased hearts. Jesus came to do radical heart surgery—to cleanse and transform us from the inside out, by the power of His death and resurrection."[4]

If God chose us, He must know something about us that we don't. Besides, says Billy Graham, "How happy would a parent be if his child constantly questioned him as to whether his needs would be met?"

That's kind of a scary thought. We can be selfish for constantly questioning God's love. He just wants us to be honest with Him—*finally!*

I think forgiving yourself is a huge stumbling block for myself and others. It is hard to forgive myself, to allow myself to move on, to not wonder if people (old friends) judge me for what I did. I feel like I still don't deserve forgiveness. But that's obviously not the way God works. It's not really about me—it's about God's character and His inability to be like man: fickle, petty, conditional. I have to trust that and let Him define me, not my actions or relationship history. —Katie, 29

Baby Jesus Faith

You hear all kinds of things in Sunday school. Earlier you read about Jonah and the whale, and now I'd like to share about childlike faith from the perspective of baby Jesus. When Jesus was a child, His parents traveled in what I can only consider to be a modern-day carpool. Amidst friends and relatives, they all traveled on foot to visit the temple and make their annual sacrifices. Jesus went with them, but this year was *different*. When it was time to leave, He stayed behind. He listened. He asked questions (Luke 2:46). Three days later, after frantic searching Mary and Joseph finally found Jesus.

And you know what happens? Jesus *rebukes* them for asking where He was! "'Why were you searching for me?' he asked. 'Didn't you know I had to be in my Father's house?'" (Luke 2:49).

I'm assuming this shocked Mary and Joseph. Jesus's parents didn't understand…yet. Obviously they knew their child was special. (Not every pregnancy is preceded by angelic visits!) Yet they reacted in fear when their child went missing. They panicked. They didn't get it.

Later on in His ministry Jesus prayed, "I praise you, Father, Lord of heaven and earth, because you have hidden these things from the wise and learned, and revealed them to little children" (Matthew 11:25). We think "Sunday school answers" are too simplistic, but they're really deeply profound.

I hope you see this as an encouragement. Saying we should have faith like a child's isn't meant to make you feel bad for being a grownup. It doesn't mean that you're not young enough, or that you don't have enough faith. Even Jesus's parents felt more like the child in this situation. If you can learn to treat each person around you as a fellow child of God, maybe, just maybe, you'll start to understand how to forgive. Maybe it will cause you to treat others with more kindness.

Everyone knows the story of the ugly duckling. You know—the odd one out. He was different from the other ducklings. Imperfect. That's how one of Jesus's apostles viewed himself. But this apostle, Paul, refused to feel sorry for himself *because* he wasn't perfect.

Say what?

The Least of These

Paul knew his story was less than perfect. Before his conversion, he persecuted Christians! But he didn't let the sins of the past stop him from becoming a mighty Christ-follower. He received the title of apostle because he wasn't afraid to truly let God transform him. He gave his weaknesses to God and became a new man. The former enemy of Christians became one of the most influential leaders of the early church.

> For I am the least of all the apostles. In fact, I'm not even worthy to be called an apostle after the way I persecuted God's church. But whatever I am now, it is all because God poured out his special favor on me—and not without results (1 Corinthians 15:9-10 NLT).

When we beat ourselves over the head about our shortcomings, mistakes, and even what we assume to be failures, remember all those imperfect people who made it into the "Hall of Faith." Remember those who have gone before us.

- Peter denied Jesus three times.
- Abraham slept with his servant.
- Paul persecuted Christians.
- Jonah ran away from God's call.

You've made mistakes. So have I. But *we can move forward.* Christ can transform you and me—just like He transformed Paul. Proverbs 26:11 says that "As a dog returns to its vomit, so fools repeat their folly." Don't be a fool, caught forever in the trap of the same old mistakes. You might be weak. You might be humble. But with the power of God within you, you can choose a new life. Just look what happened to those Bible characters.

- Peter became the rock on which Christ built His church.
- Abraham became the father of many nations.
- Paul became a great missionary and wrote many of the New Testament epistles.
- Jonah went to Nineveh and helped save the city from destruction.

What's the similarity between these men? They all had a choice, and they chose obedience. Remember, the only person you have control over is *yourself.* The only attitude you can control is your own. We can't control what other people do, how they act, or what they feel. We can only make choices for ourselves.

Today, choose obedience to God's call—just like Peter, Abraham, Paul, and Jonah!

Not Your Sin

Sometimes God uses sin to force us to start over. It reminds me of a story in the book of Joshua. The nation of Israel had "violated the instructions about the things set apart for the Lord. A man named

Achan had stolen some of these dedicated things, so the LORD was very angry with the Israelites" (Joshua 7:1 NLT).

Joshua, the Israelites' leader, didn't know about this treachery. Instead of checking in with God before going to battle, Joshua gave orders to send out the troops to the city of Ai. This was after the famous Battle of Jericho when God told the Israelites to march around the city for seven days. Strange orders, but they were victorious. With God's help, the Israelites were getting used to winning.

So what was it about this battle that was so different? The soldiers of Ai defeated the Israelites soundly, killing 36 men. It wasn't until after the defeat that Joshua asked God what was up. That was when he learned that Achan had stolen a robe, 200 silver coins, and a bar of gold weighing more than a pound from Babylon (Joshua 7:21). If Joshua had prayed earlier, he might have prevented the defeat.

Without realizing it, you may be in a similar situation.

> Then Joshua cried out, "Oh, Sovereign LORD, why did you bring us across the Jordan River if you are going to let the Amorites kill us? If only we had been content to stay on the other side!" (Joshua 7:7 NLT).

What's next? After confessing sin and turning around you may still be experiencing pain. It feels like your trial is far from over. Maybe it's just getting started. *God might be pruning you.* L.B. Cowman said in one of my favorite devotional books, *Streams in the Desert,* "To burn brightly our lives must first experience the flame. In other words, we cease to bless others when we cease to bleed."[5]

There may be areas in your life you have not yielded to Christ. It could be your pride or the way you act toward those less fortunate than you. Bruce Wilkinson said in his book *Secrets of the Vine,* "God's strategy for coaxing a greater harvest out of His branches is not the one you and I would prefer. His plan is to prune, which means to thin, to reduce, to cut off. As unthinkable as it sounds—as contradictory as it is—the Vinedresser's secret for more is…less."[6]

Sometimes our sufferings have *nothing* to do with you and everything to do with others' actions. Like Joshua, you believed it was *your* fault. It wasn't until the guilty party had been punished that God allowed Israel to be victorious again.

Today, I want you to ask the question. Are you suffering as a result of others' sin?

This is a difficult question to ask. The answer might not come right away—and neither will an end to your pain. *Hang in there.*

Ask God to keep you accountable to help you see *your* blind spots and uncover *your* sin. Ask Him to get it out and destroy it before it hurts others. Your name may be bitter and you may feel like an outcast, but God will provide, bless your obedience, and give you hope. As Pastor Chris Brown puts it, "The best new chapters begin with faith and honesty."[7]

Ask God to help you forgive those around you who may have hurt you without realizing it. You may feel like the odd man out. You may even feel like they deserve to die (like Achan) for their cover-up.

Ask God for the same measure of grace to use on yourself for being less than perfect. God cares about you. Stop comparing yourself to others. God loves you because He created you and there is no one else like you. Don't waste His grace today.

If you take away nothing more from this chapter, or even this book, remember that God *loves* sinners like you and me. Isn't that crazy to think that God desires and even craves our love? Even when we're totally incapable, struggling, and hiding in our sin? He accepts what we can give Him—even if it's just *phileo* love, like Peter—and that, my friend, is a good place to start!

Jonah 1:3 says, "Jonah ran away from the LORD." Have you ever tried to run away from a command God was clearly giving to you?

Hosea 6:1-3 says, "Come, let us return to the LORD. He has torn us to pieces but he will heal us; he has injured us but he will bind up our wounds." Have you ever felt like God has allowed trials to break you so that He could build you back up again? Do you feel like this is something you're going through currently?

Second Timothy 3:16 says, "All Scripture is God-breathed and is useful for teaching, rebuking, correcting and training in righteousness." Have you heard God speak to you through the Word? If so, which verse(s)? If you haven't yet, please write down a prayer asking God to use His Word to speak directly to you today.

Isaiah 43:19 says, "See, I am doing a new thing! Now it springs up; do you not perceive it?" When was the last time God did something new in your life? Were you scared? Did it hurt? What was the final outcome?

John 21:15 says, "When they had finished eating, Jesus said to Simon Peter, 'Simon son of John, do you love me more than these?'" When was the last time God asked you a tough question? What was it and how did you respond?

Romans 15:1 says, "We who are strong ought to bear with the failings of the weak and not to please ourselves." When do you find it difficult to believe God's truths? How do you help others who are struggling to believe as well?

Matthew 19:14 says, "Let the little children come to me, and do not hinder them, for the kingdom of heaven belongs to such as these." How do you exercise childlike faith?

Job 40:4 says, "I am unworthy—how can I reply to you? I put my hand over my mouth." Have you ever felt like you don't measure up? Do you feel your shortcomings or mistakes keep you from living the life God has for you?

CHAPTER 5

Get Rid of It

Have you ever realized that a "test of faith" doesn't really test anything unless it pushes you past your last test?[1] That's something I've been learning recently.

It's always nice to hear everything is going to be *okay*. What no one ever wants to hear is that God is *disciplining* you.

There's absolutely no way I can talk about forgiveness without sharing a passage that impacted me greatly. Let's read it together, shall we? Open up your Bible and read from John 15:1-17. (Or read it here below.)

If you are having a hard time, I encourage you to take this breather as an opportunity to do a "spiritual inventory" on yourself. God wants us to *listen*. To be still and know that He is God (Psalm 46:10).

Just let John 15 encourage you and wash over you and your thirsty soul. If you don't have a Bible handy you can read it here:

> I am the true vine, and my Father is the gardener. He cuts off every branch in me that bears no fruit, while every branch that does bear fruit he prunes so that it will be even more fruitful. You are already clean because of the word I have spoken to you. Remain in me, as I also remain in you.

No branch can bear fruit by itself; it must remain in the vine. Neither can you bear fruit unless you remain in me.

I am the vine; you are the branches. If you remain in me and I in you, you will bear much fruit; apart from me you can do nothing. If you do not remain in me, you are like a branch that is thrown away and withers; such branches are picked up, thrown into the fire and burned. If you remain in me and my words remain in you, ask whatever you wish, and it will be done for you. This is to my Father's glory, that you bear much fruit, showing yourselves to be my disciples.

As the Father has loved me, so have I loved you. Now remain in my love. If you keep my commands, you will remain in my love, just as I have kept my Father's commands and remain in his love. I have told you this so that my joy may be in you and that your joy may be complete. My command is this: Love each other as I have loved you. Greater love has no one than this: to lay down one's life for one's friends. You are my friends if you do what I command. I no longer call you servants, because a servant does not know his master's business. Instead, I have called you friends, for everything that I learned from my Father I have made known to you. You did not choose me, but I chose you and appointed you to go and bear fruit—fruit that will last—and so that whatever you ask in my name the Father will give you. This is my command: Love each other.

After reading, ask yourself only *one* question: Could God be disciplining me?

Is God allowing your life to come to a screeching halt because of unconfessed sin? Did you do something to offend someone else? Maybe someone hurt you and it stings? Or maybe you can't forgive yourself because of the choices *you* made! Either way, I want you to know that God loves you and because He loves you, *He will discipline you!* No gardener lets a vine grow whatever way it sees fit. Nor did anyone say following Jesus and being His disciple was easy. The gardener wants you to flourish in abundance, and there is no way He can continue to help you bear fruit if you are *disobedient*. Do *not* be afraid to ask God to show you what you did wrong. If the pain in your life is a direct result of sin, once you confess your sin to God *you are free!* It's that simple. Do *not* let the devil drag you down in thinking there is no way out. If God sets you free, you are truly free (John 8:36). I *urge* you right now to write down a prayer below and ask God to set you free. Friends, don't turn another page until you've completed this section!

The Wrong Answer

I want you to re-read John 15:1-17, and this time I want you to answer three questions.

Is God disciplining me?

Is God pruning me?

Is God asking me to remain in forgiveness?

Fellow author and friend Lisa Velthouse said forgiveness isn't always the right answer. As she puts it, "Forgiveness is the wrong answer when the actual answer is lovingly confronting sin in another person's life. If someone has hurt you as a result of unchecked sin patterns in their life, calling that sin to their attention might be the appropriate response. Obeying biblical commands to forgive doesn't mean every offense should easily roll off our backs, unchecked."

Don't get frustrated if the answers don't reveal themselves right away, but if you are willing and open I believe God will honor you with an answer. For instance, if the answer is your suffering is *discipline* due to your sin, after you repent the trial should stop. If it continues and you find yourself harboring the same old bitterness with mixed emotions, then it could mean that God is pruning you. Remember, it's *because* God loves you so much He wants you to be even more fruitful. Often, it's during this process where we have the most struggle.

The future is a blank slate that God is writing on. How can I know what I'll feel tomorrow? As for hope, my hope is in God. People fail. As long as my hope is in the right place, how can I lose? —Marie, 24

Have you ever seen the short Pixar film called *Boundin'*? It's the story of a lamb who is so in love with his white coat that he dances for the neighbor animals...until the farmer shears him. He's so embarrassed.

Pink even. When a jackalope comes along and tells the lamb to dance regardless of whether he is sheared (exposed) or not, the lamb realizes he still has four good legs and learns. He learns to dance through his embarrassment.

That's what God wants for us through the pruning process. My favorite part of the film is at the end when the lamb knows shearing time is coming up again. This time instead of cowering in fear when the farmer comes to snatch him, the lamb offers up his leg right away. It's that kind of attitude and repentant heart that God is looking for in you and in me.

Expectations, Schmexpectations

Expectations are *the* worst. Especially when you're waiting on the other person to apologize. Sometimes the other person will never say, "I'm sorry."

You can be waiting a long time on his or her forgiveness. Maybe it's because he's not aware of his sin. Maybe she doesn't think it's a big deal. Unmet expectations can lead to fear and frustration.

What if they never *apologize?* you wonder. *What if I bring it up and they get mad at me and don't want to talk about it anymore?*

If we're honest, we don't want to be the one to say something *first*. It's thoughts and questions like these that can easily paralyze the process of forgiveness. If not for the grace of God, we might never confront each other—to say nothing of forgiving each other! I'm reminded again of Matthew 18:15. Jesus tells us, "If your brother or sister sins, go and point out their fault, just between the two of you. If they listen to you, you have won them over."

So talk to the person you're having trouble with.

Not on social media.

Not to your best friends.

Not at the lunch tables or at the water cooler at the office.

Just you.

This is something I still struggle with. Please don't think that I'm perfect. I haven't always followed the Bible's example in Matthew on forgiveness. Sometimes I've nursed an unhealthy expectation that turned into a grudge and spiraled out of control. Unrealistic expectations lead to broken relationships.

Maybe you're dealing with a superior or a coworker and you're afraid to go to HR. Maybe you're dating a guy and he doesn't treat you right, but it's better than being single. Maybe she's your girlfriend and you don't see anything wrong with sleeping with her before marriage. When two people don't handle a situation in a healthy manner it can create strife—or, in the worst-case scenario—end the relationship. Proverbs 17:9 says, "Love prospers when a fault is forgiven, but dwelling on it separates close friends" (NLT).

You may not realize it, but your habitual sin may be the cause of death in the relationship.

While you are waiting to learn if God is asking you to remain in forgiveness, there is actually something you can do. Don't think that it's wasted time. Like the lamb, you can learn to dance again with no shame.

I am in tears remembering where I was and where I am now. I know that if I hadn't gone through what I did, I wouldn't be who I am today. I have been freed from all the hate I had for myself, my sisters, for the Christian men and women, and everyone who at some point harmed me. I chose to forgive them and set myself free from the bondage of being tied down by hate, but I didn't do it alone. God had a whole lot to do with it. I am changed and liberated. —Melany, 20

Ask yourself this: *What are my expectations during this season?*

Healthy expectations of forgiveness create boundaries. Sometimes the best thing to do is to allow some space between yourself and the offended person. Take the time to deal with the situation in private. If you find it doesn't go away, and they continually hurt you, then it's time to seek the counsel of a trusted friend or mentor and confront him or her in a loving way. I love that the Bible gives us permission to be proactive so we don't fall back into the rut of unhealthy expectations.

Spiritual Zombie

I recently read a great point about forgiveness in *Lazarus Awakening*, a personally challenging book study I recently went through with a friend. Joanna Weaver wrote, "Though there are many reasons to crucify our sinful nature, I think these may be the best: you can't tempt a dead person—or make one afraid."[2]

I am a verbal processor, so I usually seek the counsel of trusted friends or family members. I pray about the issues and I read Scripture because often the answers are right in front of me and I can see them when I am focused on the right thing.
—Shawna, 27

I've heard that before but somehow the way she talked about it *convicted* me. If I'm honest, my actions awaken a wild woman with intense desires from within—like the desire to withhold forgiveness from others. It starts with the stupidest little things. *Petty things.* Like a friend not telling me she's pregnant first before posting it for everyone to see on Facebook.

Regarding the situations in which we're suffering, Joanna asked the question, "What three things move us to feel upset, hurt, and/or fearful?"

When I couldn't think of anything major I was astonished. How can I be so oblivious that I am alive to my sins? *I should be dead.* And yet I feel like a spiritual zombie. Joanna continues, "God allowed a painful misunderstanding with friends to strip me of everything I had assumed I needed for life. Their love, their friendship, their kind understanding and support—all that was gone. And nothing I did made the situation better, only worse. The removal of their approval hurt me so deeply I thought I was going to die."[3]

Wow. *Just wow.* Isn't it amazing how the enemy knows our trigger points? Sometimes it's easy to confuse the enemy tempting us with our own pain on the matter. That's when we turn into spiritual zombies.

Refusing to let go. Refusing to forgive. Letting petty things become big things. We ignore God's command to love and forgive and be forgiven.

I have thoughts sometimes that cause me to obsess about things that are not even true, and if I choose to dwell in that, I lose that battle. I experience spiritual battle most when I fight with my husband and the same old angry words get pulled out to hurt him. —Denise, 30

Can you relate? If God says we are to be dead to sins and alive in Christ then He must have *meant* it. What turns you into a spiritual zombie? At the end of this chapter you will have the opportunity to write down your three biggest "triggers" and ask God to help you remain alive in Him.

Cherish Forgiveness

Have you ever gotten into a fight with a friend and had it end badly? It doesn't seem fair. Maybe you expected him to be there and he wasn't. Maybe you confided in her and she betrayed you. The one person you trusted the most let you down…in a *big* way. Now the friendship is over and you're left wondering what happened. Maybe you said some harsh words. Maybe you deleted this person off Facebook in haste. Because everyone knows if someone doesn't exist online they certainly don't exist in real life. *Wrong.* It's not fun to be hurt. I've been there. Many times.

I respect the friend who has the guts to come to me and apologize. Usually it's me who has to apologize first—or should.

> If I had cherished sin in my heart,
> the Lord would not have listened;
> but God has surely listened
> and has heard my prayer.
> Praise be to God,
> who has not rejected my prayer

or withheld his love from me!
(Psalm 66:18-20)

Let this psalm stop you cold. You aren't cherishing forgiveness. That's the last thing you want to hear God say about you—am I right? You have to remember what Jesus says in 1 John 4:18: "There is no fear in love. But perfect love drives out fear, because fear has to do with punishment. The one who fears is not made perfect in love."

If we fear man above God, we are in danger of sinning. The good news is we *love* (and forgive) because God loved us first (1 John 4:19). If we cannot extend the same grace and mercy God gave us, we're in trouble. Do we want God to listen and continue listening to our prayers? *Then cherish forgiveness.* Don't be a liar.

> Whoever claims to love God yet hates a brother or sister is a liar. For whoever do not love their brother and sister, whom they have seen, cannot love God, whom they have not seen (1 John 4:20).

> Continue to work out your salvation with fear and trembling, for it is God who works in you to will and to act in order to fulfill his good purpose (Philippians 2:12-13).

You say that it's impossible? Maybe this person acted like a Christian before he or she stabbed you in the back. Maybe you've told the story a hundred times. Maybe you've even told God a hundred *times* a hundred. Now what?

When at the depths of depression I find it best to process my feelings with family and friends. —Jessica, 26

Watch Yourself!

I hope the suffering you are currently going through can teach you how to overcome past hurts, future fears, and present circumstances.

I want you to know that you're not alone. Hurting alone is just plain awful. I know. I've been there. For years, sprinkled throughout my writings I've shared my story of failure. How my health made me lose my mind. How the eczema took the skin from my body. I never thought God—or a man—could ever truly love me. I've been hesitating to share this story because it was so long ago, and I've shared bits and pieces in my first two books.

Here goes nothing.

When I dated Jake (not his real name), I thought God was telling me he was the one for me. I was going to spend the rest of my life with him. Even Jake felt this way. He told me things I longed to hear one day from my future husband. He said I was only person for him and how glad he was that I'd waited for him all those years to finally come around. I didn't know the difference between being pursued and pursuing others until *after* Jake and I broke up. It took me a few years to let go of all the bitterness against him and his hypocritical words. I wrote Jake nasty letter after nasty letter. I called him out. I told him he wasn't being godly and how badly he had hurt me and shattered my hopes of a future into a million pieces.

> If your brother or sister sins against you, rebuke them; and
> if they repent, forgive them. Even if they sin again you
> seven times in a day and seven times come back to you say-
> ing "I repent," you must forgive them (Luke 17:3-4).

With that same measure of grace and forgiveness we receive from God, I had to forgive Jake. I think the hardest part for me was how much stock I had put in our future together. Now that Jake was out of the picture, I felt I literally had no future. I couldn't see the red flags, warning signs, or wisdom that others were trying to speak into my life before we broke up. I was only going to see what I wanted to see, listen to the people I wanted to listen to...and it was all part of my downfall. Have you been there?

Days went by before I could stop crying. I cried so many tears that the eczema on my feet actually spread to my face. Jake was the reason for the biggest health crisis in my life. I lost the skin off my face and ended up in the hospital. All because I couldn't get over a boy. I just couldn't get over the fact that I had ruined the rest of my life.

I didn't speak to my father for a year because I didn't want to forgive him for cheating on my mom. I had to trust *God* to deal with the situation instead of trying to make things right by holding out love. I went over to my father's house and sat down with him and his new wife. I told them that whether they were sorry or not, I forgave them for their actions and for hurting me. And then I asked them if they would forgive me for how I dealt with the situation. They have never apologized, but I now have a better relationship with my dad. —Megan, 25

Or so I thought.

It didn't take me long after I got out of the hospital to make amends with my family and friends who I had pushed away, thinking I had my future all figured out with Jake. I even had my mom drive down to the dumpster and get rid of all the pictures and physical remnants that reminded me of our failed relationship. After that, I was free from bitterness...but I had a long road of recovery ahead.

Forgiveness doesn't just affect relationships, but the body, soul, mind, and strength. It took my body ten years to heal from that health crash. I don't know why God didn't step in and heal me. But because God allowed my rash to spread I have an even bigger story to tell—one that doesn't just end with forgiveness but restoration.

Thankfully, Jake came to me a few years after I had gotten rid of all my bitterness against him—after I had started rebuilding a new life. He apologized and asked me to forgive him. I still have that letter in a journal as a reminder of God's love for me. So my question for you is this: *Do you have the courage to forgive the person who hurt you the most?*

We all have relationships that require extra grace. That's why Jesus tells us to forgive many times. If I can't learn to forgive others, am I really living the abundant life Jesus promised? Jesus said, "I have come that they may have life, and have it to the full" (John 10:10).

I won't tell you how or when to forgive. Only God can do that. Yes, there has been suffering in your life. It has devastated you and reaped severe consequences over your life. But I hope you will pray and allow God to cleanse your heart so that you can forgive those He has brought into your life today.

The Box

I don't know about you, but every time I think I have God figured out, I find out I don't. God doesn't live in a box. Because of Christ's death on the cross we have access to the power of the Holy Spirit, and with the Spirit's help we are free.

We need the Spirit because our human weapons aren't much good in spiritual battle. We arm ourselves with emotion—but our emotions can be totally misleading. We arm ourselves with information—but our mind traps us into believing half-truths until we're totally deceived.

> We use God's mighty weapons, not worldly weapons, to knock down the strongholds of human reasoning and to destroy false arguments (2 Corinthians 10:4 NLT).

Recently, I was super emotional over something my husband did. I know Marc didn't *mean* to hurt me, but somehow I took offense. My mind couldn't stop going back to *the box*. All the past lies I previously believed and let define who I was popped out. I *thought* I had given them to God. Turns out some wounds just grow in bigger boxes. Hidden ones. I cried out to God to help me destroy that box once and for all. I wanted to smash it to pieces. I didn't want to live in the hurt and unforgiveness of my past, and I didn't want to harbor unforgiveness against my husband in the present. When I asked God to help me, His Spirit led me to Isaiah 1:18. Once again God knocked me out of the box I put Him and myself in.

> "Come now, let's settle this," says the LORD. "Though your sins are like scarlet, I will make them as white as snow. Though they are red like crimson, I will make them as white as wool" (Isaiah 1:18 NLT).

I love that God knows when we're hurting. He constantly pursues us because He wants us to be set free. He breaks us out of those boxes.

Get Rid of the Box

Recently, my husband bought us a home with a huge front yard. Unfortunately, the yard wasn't in great shape. Bermuda grass—a weed here in California—had choked out the rest of the lawn. As soon as we moved in, the Home Owners Association sent us a letter saying we had thirty days to get our lawn in order. Before we could start growing new grass, we had to spend two weeks letting the weed killer go to work on the Bermuda grass so we could dig it up properly—*roots and all*. We wanted to make sure the weeds would never come back again.

It's the same with forgiveness. You can't just treat the symptoms—you have to go to the source. You have to dig out the roots. James 1:21 puts it this way: "So get rid of all the filth and evil in your lives, and humbly accept the word God has planted in your hearts, for it has the power to save your souls" (NLT).

When I literally took God at His Word, He healed me. Remember my Jake story? The verse God used to prompt me to get rid of my shoebox full of memories was *this* verse. He promised me if I got rid of this box and put aside all the bitterness it represented, *He would be strong enough to save me.*

It was a risk. I could have waited…but I'm so glad I didn't hesitate. Partial obedience, after all, is still disobedience. When God asks us to do something we need to obey immediately.

Do you know the story of King Saul and the prophet Samuel? God gave instructions to King Saul to completely destroy the Amalekites. It was important that Saul destroy everything *totally*. Nothing and no one was to be spared. Read what King Saul does below, in 1 Samuel 15:10-25:

> Then the word of the LORD came to Samuel: "I am grieved that I have made Saul king, because he has turned away from me and has not carried out my instructions." Samuel was troubled, and he cried out to the LORD all that night.

Early in the morning Samuel got up and went to meet Saul, but he was told, "Saul has gone to Carmel. There he has set up a monument in his own honor and has turned and gone on down to Gilgal."

When Samuel reached him, Saul said, "The LORD bless you! I have carried out the LORD's instructions."

But Samuel said, "What then is this bleating of sheep in my ears? What is this lowing of cattle that I hear?"

Saul answered, "The soldiers brought them from the Amalekites; they spared the best of the sheep and cattle to sacrifice to the LORD your God, but we totally destroyed the rest."

"Enough!" Samuel said to Saul. "Let me tell you what the LORD said to me last night."

"Tell me," Saul replied.

Samuel said, "Although you were once small in your own eyes, did you not become the head of the tribes of Israel? The LORD anointed you king over Israel. And he sent you on a mission, saying, 'Go and completely destroy those wicked people, the Amalekites; wage war against them until you have wiped them out.' Why did you not obey the LORD? Why did you pounce on the plunder and do evil in the eyes of the LORD?"

"But I did obey the LORD," Saul said. "I went on the mission the LORD assigned me. I completely destroyed the Amalekites and brought back Agag their king. The soldiers took sheep and cattle from the plunder, the best of what was devoted to God, in order to sacrifice them to the LORD your God at Gilgal."

But Samuel replied: "Does the LORD delight in burnt offerings and sacrifices as much as in obeying the voice of the LORD? To obey is better than sacrifice, and to heed is better than the fat of rams. For rebellion is like the sin of divination, and arrogance like the evil of idolatry. Because you have rejected the word of the LORD, he has rejected you as king."

Then Saul said to Samuel, "I have sinned. I violated

the LORD's command and your instructions. I was afraid of the people and so I gave in to them. Now I beg you, forgive my sin and come back with me, so that I may worship the LORD."

Saul had two chances to ask for God's forgiveness. Each time he justified his disobedience. Gave an excuse. Did you catch that? Samuel's response sums up what God wants from you and from me: *To obey is better than sacrifice.*

Now enter David. He had waited a very long time under the dark shadow of King Saul. After God rejected Saul, he had Samuel the prophet anoint David to be the next king. Many years passed and David finally became king. But he wasn't perfect either. After David sinned with Bathsheba and had her husband killed to disguise his adultery, it was his turn to be confronted by a prophet—this time the prophet Nathan. Read what happens in 2 Samuel 12:1-13.

> The LORD sent Nathan to David. When he came to him, he said, "There were two men in a certain town, one rich and the other poor. The rich man had a very large number of sheep and cattle, but the poor man had nothing except one little ewe lamb he had bought. He raised it, and it grew up with him and his children. It shared his food, drank from his cup and even slept in his arms. It was like a daughter to him.
>
> "Now a traveler came to the rich man, but the rich man refrained from taking one of his own sheep or cattle to prepare a meal for the traveler who had come to him. Instead, he took the ewe lamb that belonged to the poor man and prepared it for the one who had come to him."
>
> David burned with anger against the man and said to Nathan, "As surely as the LORD lives, the man who did this deserves to die! He must pay for that lamb four times over, because he did such a thing and had no pity."
>
> Then Nathan said to David, "You are the man! This is what the LORD, the God of Israel, says: 'I anointed you king over Israel, and I delivered you from the hand of Saul.

I gave your master's house to you, and your master's wives into your arms. I gave you all Israel and Judah. And if all this had been too little, I would have given you even more. Why did you despise the word of the Lord by doing what is evil in his eyes? You struck down Uriah the Hittite with the sword and took his wife to be your own. You killed him with the sword of the Ammonites. Now, therefore, the sword will never depart from your house, because you despised me and took the wife of Uriah the Hittite to be your own.'

"This is what the Lord says: 'Out of your own household I am going to bring calamity upon you. Before your very eyes I will take your wives and give them to one who is close to you, and he will sleep with your wives in broad daylight. You did it in secret, but I will do this thing in broad daylight before all Israel.'"

Then David said to Nathan, "I have sinned against the Lord."

Nathan replied, "The Lord has taken away your sin. You are not going to die."

No excuses. David admitted his sin and because he didn't try to hide it, God forgave him.

Friends, it's important to remember that no one is perfect. We all make mistakes. Usually it takes a person of God (like a prophet) to confront us.

What's in your box? What secret anger and bitterness are you hanging on to?

For years, I kept my fears about my health in the box. Here's the secret: *I didn't trust God to heal me.* I had cried so hard about my breakup with Jake that it messed with my entire body. I felt like it was *my* fault that I was suffering, and because of that I expected to suffer the consequences...*alone.*

That's when I remembered James 1:21—"Get rid of all moral filth and the evil that is so prevalent and humbly accept the word planted in you, which can save you." God told me to act quickly once again.

He told me to get rid of all the creams and medications which, at that point, were the only thing saving my skin and my sanity. *I obeyed.* I got it all out from underneath my bed, put it in a black trash bag, and asked my mom to dump it in some dumpster. I didn't want to know where she was putting it so there would be no way for me to look back!

That's twice God asked for my box, and twice I obeyed. Thankfully, I had an understanding and loving mom who was willing to get down and dirty to help me be free from the sin that so easily entangled me.

God is not afraid of our sin either. He's not afraid of whatever you've got laid away in that secret box. Give it to Him today.

Matthew 18:15 says, "If your brother or sister sins, go and point out their fault, just between the two of you. If they listen to you, you have won them over." Have you always been obedient to this command? What are the consequences of disobeying it?

Proverbs 4:25-27 says, "Let your eyes look straight ahead; fix your gaze directly before you. Give careful thought to the paths for your feet and be steadfast in all your ways. Do not turn to the right or the left; keep your foot from evil." What are your biggest "triggers"? What keeps you from walking alive in Christ and dead to the world?

Colossians 3:13 says, "Bear with each other and forgive one another if any of you has a grievance against someone. Forgive as the Lord forgave you." What is more difficult for you—asking for forgiveness or being asked? Why?

First Peter 5:7 says, "Cast all your anxiety on him because he cares for you." Do you have any boxes of hate, unforgiveness, lies, or false expectations that you're still holding on to? What would it take for you to give them to God?

Hebrews 12:1-2 says, "Since we are surrounded by such a great cloud of witnesses, let us throw off everything that hinders and the sin that so easily entangles. And let us run with perseverance the race marked out for us, fixing our eyes on Jesus, the pioneer and perfecter of faith. For the joy set before him he endured the cross, scorning its shame, and sat down at the right hand of the throne of God." Is there any unforgiveness in your past you need to get rid of? How does it still affect your life today?

PART 3

FORGIVEN

If you forgive other people when they sin against you,
your heavenly Father will also forgive you.
But if you do not forgive others their sins,
your Father will not forgive your sins.

MATTHEW 6:14-15

CHAPTER 6

Unbound

Initially, I wanted to open this chapter with the statement that there are two kinds of people—those who are imprisoned by others' actions and those who are imprisoned by their own actions. Too bad. I *immediately* felt convicted. When we try to put people or circumstances into categories and judge them according to *our* standards we endanger ourselves. We don't always see everything or know everything that's going on, and our wisdom is *not* superior to God's.

There is a story in the Bible that helped open my eyes to His truth.

> As he went along, he saw a man blind from birth. His disciples asked him, "Rabbi, who sinned, this man or his parents, that he was born blind?"
>
> "Neither this man nor his parents sinned," said Jesus, "but this happened so that the works of God might be displayed in his life. As long as it is day, we must do the works of him who sent me. Night is coming, when no one can work. While I am in the world, I am the light of the world."
>
> After saying this, he spit on the ground, made some mud with the saliva, and put it on the man's eyes. "Go," he

told him, "wash in the Pool of Siloam" (this word means "Sent"). So the man went and washed, and came home seeing (John 9:1-7).

Every morning you wake up and there is some new problem. You might feel stuck in your very own personal hell. The longer you try and fight this, the longer the Lord lovingly allows an extraordinary trial to stay. Wait, *seriously?* You must choose to believe that He loves you and trust that He is going to take care of your needs.

At one point in my life I felt so completely unlovable I thought I was worthless. Remembering how much I have been forgiven humbles me and makes it possible for me to be forgiving towards others. In fact, no matter what sin they have committed against me, I can forgive them because of what I have been forgiven.
—Phoebe, 28

That story about Jesus healing a blind man isn't the only story like that in the Gospels. Check out this one in Luke 18:35-43:

> As Jesus approached Jericho, a blind man was sitting by the roadside begging. When he heard the crowd going by, he asked what was happening. They told him, "Jesus of Nazareth is passing by."
>
> He called out, "Jesus, Son of David, have mercy on me!"
>
> Those who led the way rebuked him and told him to be quiet, but he shouted all the more, "Son of David, have mercy on me!"
>
> Jesus stopped and ordered the man to be brought to him. When he came near, Jesus asked him, "What do you want me to do for you?"
>
> "Lord, I want to see," he replied.
>
> Jesus said to him, "Receive your sight; your faith has healed you." Immediately he received his sight and

followed Jesus, praising God. When all the people saw it,
they also praised God.

Both blind men were healed—one with mud and spit, and one just
by the word of Jesus. I think God wanted to show that there is more
than one way to be set free! So why is it so scary when God asks you, just
like He asked the blind beggar, "What do you want me to do for you?"

Maybe you want to be healed from a broken heart, a negative bank
account, or a church split. And you want to be healed *right now*! The
hard part is waiting for the answer to come. Paul gives great encouragement when he writes, "Do not throw away your confidence; it will
be richly rewarded. You need to persevere so that when you have done
the will of God, you will receive what he has promised" (Hebrews
10:35-36).

Don't look at the number of days, months, or years it takes for God
to listen and answer you. Do not throw away *all* your confidence. During this process, you may feel blind in that you cannot see what God
is up to. You feel like passing blame and finding fault, but He is up to
something. I promise you that.

What Do You Really Want?

I want to highlight that second blind man again. He received what
he wanted so badly from the Lord. Not only did his confidence pay off,
but he was also shown love from Jesus Himself! The crowd kept yelling at the man to be quiet, but he only shouted louder.

Have you ever felt like this man? I have. You know Jesus can hear
you, but for whatever reason the crowds of this life try to choke you
and keep you from crying out. In those times, remember this: *Anguish
leads to a powerful prayer life*. Don't let Satan make you believe otherwise. When Jesus finally heard the man He *stopped*. Yes, that's right. He
looked right into his eyes—which could not yet see—and asked the
man, "What do you want Me to do for you?"

What a powerful question. Thankfully this man didn't hesitate.
Instead of telling Jesus his sob story or trying to explain the reasons
why he was blind, he simply asked.

You can do that too. You can just ask. We have that ability through the power of prayer. In *One Year Alone with God,* Ava Pennington writes, "Intercessory prayer causes us to look beyond our interests as we become aware of the needs and burdens of others...Intercessory prayer is critical if we are having difficulty forgiving someone else. It is almost impossible to stay angry with a person when we ask God to help us see them through His perspective, and pray for Him to bless them abundantly!"[1]

We might think prayer helps change God or speed up the process of healing, but in fact, it changes you! Just like the two blind men, we need more than physical healing. We need to see God and experience His forgiveness!

Let's Make a Deal

There are a few examples in the Bible of what happens when people try to make a deal while waiting on God to come through for them. The first example is Eve. "Eat an apple and you won't die," said the serpent. She believed him. She grabbed the fruit, ate it, and even shared the deal with Adam. As a result sin entered into the world.

Our second example is Jesus. Years later, Christ, or the "last Adam," came on the scene to redeem their deal. Failure was not an option. He encountered Satan, the king of dealmakers, during His forty days in the desert. Three times the enemy tried to make a deal, and three times the Lord told him no.

At first the deal Satan was offering seemed harmless. Jesus had been fasting, and the devil told Him to transform stones into bread. He must have been hungry, after all. But Jesus wouldn't do it. You don't make deals with Satan.

The deals got increasingly more tempting, but each time Jesus rejected Satan's lies.

I love that Jesus is the only one who successfully stood up to temptation without sinning. Jesus refused to cling to His rights (Philippians 2:6). He *never* made a deal with the devil.

The third example is Hannah. Each year she and her family traveled to make sacrifices to the Lord. She was bullied by her husband's other wife for having no children. I can't even imagine Hannah's anguish. In that culture a woman's worth was in the number of children she had— especially male children. Hannah had none. So she made a vow to God. (Not the enemy.) She said, "O LORD of Heaven's Armies, if you will look upon my sorrow and answer my prayer and give me a son, then I will give him back to you. He will be yours for his entire lifetime, and as a sign that he has been dedicated to the LORD, his hair will never be cut" (1 Samuel 1:11 NLT).

I love that Hannah didn't make a rash decision. She counted the cost beforehand and left the outcome to God. Through her sorrow and deep anguish, God answered her prayers and she gave birth to a son named Samuel. Hannah followed through. She gave him up to God and allowed him to be educated as a priest. God used her deal to make Samuel one of Israel's most famous and just judges. He stands ready to do the same for us.

Would you or I follow through as Hannah did…and with a deal that large? Before you go to bed tonight or wake up tomorrow morning, give your heavy heart to God. Count the cost before making a deal. Maybe you just need to have faith and continue to wait on His promises. In your desperation, give your anguish to God, for He is the God who sees you. Remember what I said earlier about how anguish leads to a powerful prayer life?

In my immaturity I used to put ultimatums on God all the time—"If You are there and You can hear me, make that boy like me" or "If You are there, give me a record deal even though I've never sung in public before"…you know, really ridiculous things. Of course, when they didn't happen I could fall back on the fact that (a) He wasn't really there or (b) I wasn't asking in the right way. —Suzanne, 29

You're Insane

So let's say you've refrained from making deals. You're patiently waiting on God to show you how to forgive those who have put you in prison. Einstein says, "The definition of insanity is doing something over and over again and expecting different results."

Does that sound like your life? When you go through an incredibly hard trial, it can actually feel like God slighted you. For whatever reason the other person hasn't asked for your forgiveness. You might say things during the process like, "Haven't I already suffered enough?"

See! I know I'm not the only believer who feels like they're going insane. The process of forgiveness can make you feel like you've suffered.

But it's one thing to know the character of Christ, and another to rest in Him. It's one thing to know the cliché verses, and another to entrust your life.

That's the whole point about our trials. They're scary and they force us to survey our lives. Maybe you have been down a similar road before. Instead of trusting in God to help you navigate the path of forgiveness, you rely on your own strength. *It happens.* We need to move beyond our human reactions of selfishness, hurt, and pride. It isn't easy, but there's no other way around it.

I've learned over my short walk with the Lord that He is the one with all the power and strength. Not me. When I'm fearing men I am not fearing God, but when I fear God He gives me strength to face anything. —Denise, 30

Bullied

I've never been abused physically, but I have experienced verbal abusive from men. I want to proceed with caution because abusive situations are not pretty. Our natural tendency is to hide from shame, fear, and manipulation. These are all tactics and tricks of the enemy, Satan. He wants to keep us down in the pit of destruction. Thankfully, we serve a God who lifts us up out of the pit (Psalm 40:2).

When I researched stories on forgiveness I found a girl—we'll call her Stacy—who struggled through an abusive nightmare of epic proportions with her sister. I'll let her tell the story.

> After my sister went through a very abusive relationship, I
> had to make a choice to forgive her abuser or the bitterness
> would become too much. It was hard to find the balance
> between forgiving him and protecting her—I wanted to
> make sure I never made what he did seem okay or accept-
> able in any way, shape, or form. She needed to know more
> than anything that she was worth more, loved more, and
> stronger than she ever thought.

Nothing Stacy said and did could have prevented the situation. It went from bad to worse. Bloody blows, cops, sexual abuse, an arrest, and a restraining order make up this tall order. Her sister knew if she didn't get out of the relationship she would be killed.

The abuser had her right where he wanted her.

You can't reason with someone who struggles with abusive tendencies.

With all my heart, I want you to know forgiveness doesn't excuse the abuser. Never, ever. Instead, it frees you from *their* prison bars. Maybe you've tried rationalizing with your attacker. Don't do that. Bullies can smell fear. It's like a game to them. Whenever they catch a whiff of someone they feel is weaker or inferior to them, they go to work.

Has anyone ever made you feel inferior? Maybe someone growing up told you that your house wasn't the coolest or the biggest. Maybe a bully called you names, stole your lunch money, or robbed you of your confidence. Sticks and stones aside, words *do* hurt. But here's one thing I am sure of—*God does not tolerate abuse.* He wants us to listen to Him and act truthfully with each other. If you are Stacy or Stacy's sister in this story, I encourage you to seek out the proper authorities.

I do love that Jesus took a firm stance against the religious bullies—that is, the Pharisees, the religious leaders of the Jews. Wherever Jesus went, one thing was for sure—He radically changed people. The Pharisees didn't like it, but those considered un*cool* loved it. Why? Because they were ready and they knew they needed to change. To be healed. So they acknowledged their need for Him and Jesus healed them. I love that. That's why there are stories in the Bible about the Pharisees and how we are not to be like them. We no longer have to be afraid of being bullied around—even by the church or those in authority.

I find it hard to forgive great evil that is always rewarded. Yes, this makes it difficult—almost impossible—to love some people. —Mark, 29

Corrie ten Boom, a Dutch Christian who hid Jews during World War II and survived the horrors of the Holocaust, said, "Forgiveness is the key that unlocks the door of resentment and the handcuffs of hatred. It is the power that breaks the chains of bitterness and the shackles of selfishness."

Of all people who can say that with confidence it's Corrie. She was literally bound and thrown into the prison camps by the Nazis. But she survived, and led a great many people to Christ before she died.

Years later, long after the war, she was speaking about her experiences to a large audience. After her talk a man she recognized as one of the prison guards approached her. As hard as it was, she forgave him, understanding that "there is no pit so deep that God's love is not deeper still."

Forgiveness smells. To some people it smells like candy, hearts, and rainbows. To others it smells like death. The apostle Paul wrote something about this strong stench in 2 Corinthians 2:14-17:

> But thanks be to God, who always leads us as captives in Christ's triumphal procession and uses us to spread the aroma of the knowledge of him everywhere. For we are to God the pleasing aroma of Christ among those who are being saved and those who are perishing. To the one we are an aroma that brings death; to the other, an aroma that brings life. And who is equal to such a task? Unlike so many, we do not peddle the word of God for profit. On the contrary, in Christ we speak before God with sincerity, as those sent from God.

Corrie ten Boom is just one radical example of God walking someone through the stench of forgiveness. She refused to be bullied around by those in charge. She continued to share the message of the gospel to those around her. To those who were dying she smelled sweet. Like

Corrie, you don't have to fear your worst-case scenario. God cares, gives hope, and forgives. Not only did He extend forgiveness to those who asked Him into their hearts before dying at the hands of the Nazi Germans, but also to the bully guards who were the instruments of this torture.

Forgiveness Is a Gift

After Corrie came home from the death camp, she realized that her life was a gift from God. She was the only person in her family to make it out alive, and she outlived her father, brother, sister, and nephew.

It's one thing to share Corrie's story and another to share my own pitiful story. Although I grew up in a Christian home, I struggled with giving and receiving love. It took my dad years to express his love for me. When I was in my early twenties, I tearfully sat down with him and told him that because of his lack of emotion I couldn't feel God's love. I forgave him even though nothing changed...*at first.*

That wasn't the only problem I had. My mom took care of me through my skin and anxiety issues. The lowest day of my life was when I told her, "I would rather be homeless than live with you."

Ouch. I still can't believe I really said that. Our sharp disagreement happened over which doctor she thought I should go to. I couldn't understand why she wanted me to go back to the doctor who, I thought, had cost me years of my life. She couldn't understand why he couldn't find a way to help.

I was unaware that my mom held on to grief. It wasn't until years later that she told me the whole story from her perspective. Because I was her daughter, she took my suffering personally, wishing she could take it on herself. Gratefully, I told my mom that God could have stepped in at any point and healed me. It's because He didn't right away that I am the person I am today.

Forgiveness is a gift. When I asked my parents to forgive me I gave them a gift. I no longer held their grief against them. I had to let it go so they could let it go. I just wish I hadn't waited so long to forgive them.

But what about Corrie? She gave the man who tortured her a gift— her forgiveness.

Whenever you or I struggle with extending forgiveness, may we remember that Jesus never once got mad at the Father for His suffering. He willingly went to the cross in order to gain salvation for the world. He may have sweat blood at the thought of the torture that was ahead of Him on the cross, but He knew it was necessary to bring salvation and reconcile the world to the Father. We learn obedience by suffering, and we give the gift that is forgiveness out of the knowledge of that suffering.

> If you cling to your life, you will lose it; but if you give up your life for me, you will find it (Matthew 10:39 NLT).

What About Me?

I opened this chapter by talking about why we shouldn't judge others. But have you ever thought about *why* Christians judge each other? Until we choose not to hold on to a spirit of unforgiveness, legalism will continue. I believe unforgiveness stems from trying to compare our trials to those of others. For instance, we ask, "Why did she get off the hook while I'm left here to suffer all alone?" "Why did he get promoted at work while I got let go? It's not fair!"

Do you see the problem here? When we compare our trials to those of others we are in danger of falling into the trap door we keep hidden in our hearts. Unforgiveness plagues all of us. We usually don't see it until it's too late. We trap ourselves in the same prison we set for someone else. And *we're* the one left to suffer. *Alone.* That's the crazy part of all of this.

Corrie should have died, but she didn't. She shouldn't have forgiven the man who tortured her in the Holocaust, but she did.

What about you?

Remember the story of the unmerciful servant? You can find it in Matthew 18:21-35. A servant was in debt up to his eyeballs and the king decided to have mercy on him. The king forgave the debt and gave the man freedom. But as he was leaving the king's presence, this newly forgiven man encountered a man who owed him a couple bucks. Did he show him mercy? Nope. He had him thrown in prison. When the king found out about it he was furious.

"You evil servant! I forgave you that tremendous debt because you pleaded with me. Shouldn't you have mercy on your fellow servant, just as I had mercy on you?" Then the angry king sent the man to prison to be tortured until he had paid his entire debt (Matthew 18:32-34 NLT).

Poor servant. There's no way he'll ever get out of prison. He accepted the king's offer of mercy, but refused to extend that same mercy to a guy who owed him almost nothing.

Mercy cannot be weighed. In God's economy, we always come up short—for *all* have sinned and "all fall short of God's glorious standard" (Romans 3:23). This is nothing new. No one deserves the incredible grace and mercy of Jesus Christ. Think of that next time you think it's your place to judge your Christian brother or sister. No matter how we try to reason or compare, God's ways are not our ways, and His thoughts are higher than our thoughts (Isaiah 55:9). *Always.*

I find it hard to forgive others deeply. Shallow love is easy, but when it comes to really affirming people for who they are, it's tough to be that real. —Daron, 22

Forgive and Forget

Whenever I think of how much I am forgiven it helps me forgive others. It doesn't make forgiveness any easier, but it reminds me to not look at others' sins. If God said He removed my sins as far as the east is from the west, then why can't I forgive others? That's when I know I need to check my heart for an inner Pharisee. Jesus said, "I tell you, her sins—and they are many—have been forgiven, so she has shown me much love. But a person who is forgiven little shows only little love" (Luke 7:47 NLT).

It goes against the old proverbs that says, "Fool me once, shame on you; fool me twice, shame on me."

Forgiveness is a choice.

You might be wondering how you can care about others when you're still focused on your own pain—on the injustices someone has committed against you. You and I both need God's love to show us we're not the only ones who are suffering—even if that means doing a hard thing. Thankfully, when relationships shake the very fiber of our being, financial troubles devastate us, or roadblocks hem us in until we cry, our hope is still in Jesus. It has to be because, as Neil Anderson says, "Forgiveness is…a crisis of the will. Since God requires us to forgive, it is something we can do. (He would never require us to do something we cannot do.) Forgiveness is difficult for us because it pulls against our concept of justice."[2]

We want to get revenge. *Get even.* It's like we want to restart the relationship without losing the memory of the hurts we've suffered. But love doesn't keep any records of wrongs (1 Corinthians 13:5). That's the purest form of love, and it sure isn't easy. It's easier for me to remember every little hurtful thing someone said to me than the compliments.

I desire revenge more than justice, which I know is wrong, but it's awful to think of people "getting away" with their sins. —Brittany, 27

If you grew up in a church or went to Sunday school, at some point you heard these words: "But on the judgment day, fire will reveal what kind of work each builder has done. The fire will show if a person's work has any value" (1 Corinthians 3:13 NLT).

No more tricks. *Just fire.* When God reveals our life's work, we have to pass through the fire. Some of us will be left with rich treasures to enjoy in heaven for eternity while others will be left with straw. It's too bad the *illusionist* of this world, Satan, tries to make us believe that we can pass from this life to the next without pain. That is simply *not* the case. God cannot be deceived. Your life on this side of eternity matters. The Bible is pretty clear. We either serve the illusionist of this world or we serve God. That doesn't mean we need to carry memories of unforgiveness.

I recently watched the movie *Memento*. It's about a guy named Leonard Shelby who investigates his wife's murder. The only problem is that he's brain damaged and can't make new memories. Leonard tries to remember the situation by taking pictures, writing notes, and tattooing things he has to remember all over his body. The movie plays out backwards so you, the viewer, can't remember what's happened either. It's a slow, painful process.

"I'm not a killer," Leonard says. "I'm just someone who wanted to make things right. Can't I just let myself forget what you've told me? Can't I just let myself forget what you've made me do?"

Forgiveness is letting go. Often the hardest part is refusing to use the incredible memory capacity God gave us against others. Choose to surrender your rights of entitlement to the memory of someone else's sin. As Gary Chapman says in his book *The Five Love Languages,* "Love doesn't erase the past, but it makes the future different."[3]

The Other Side...of Forgiveness

In Numbers 32, the tribes of Reuben, Gad, and the half-tribe of Manasseh came to Moses with a request. The people of Israel were getting ready to cross the Jordan River and enter the land of Canaan...but they didn't want to go. The lands on the east of the Jordan were good for livestock, and they were perfectly content to stay where they were. "'If we have found favor in your eyes,' they said, 'let this land be given to your servants as our possession. Do not make us cross the Jordan,'" (Numbers 32:5).

Moses was uneasy about it, but once the tribes promised that they would still fight in Israel's wars, he allowed them to settle on the eastern bank.

Hundreds of years later, when Jesus visited "the region of the Gadarenes" (the descendants of the tribe of Gad), He was met by two demon-possessed men. Jesus set the men free from the demons...at which point the entire town came out to meet Jesus and *begged* Him to go away and leave them alone (Matthew 8:28-34). All those years of staying put...and look where it got them.

Can you believe that?

The grass isn't always greener on the other side, but God promises to be with us wherever we go. Even if the path is uncertain, we can trust that He'll be at our side.

Trials aren't there to break your faith. God allows them to grow our character. He takes us through the wilderness to show us what we're made of. To show us that in His strength, we are *capable*. God exposes sin so we can forgive and learn how to move on to the other side.

Jesus's disciples had to cross over to the other side of the Sea of Galilee. While they were on the water a huge storm came up and threatened to sink them. They were afraid for their lives...*until* Jesus woke up and calmed the storm. Had they not been willing to get in the boat, the disciples would never have witnessed the miracle. These new followers of Jesus encountered a faith they had never known because they were willing to take the first step and cross to the other side.

When we refuse to cross over, to finish what we started, to allow God's perfect work through our trials, we are actually being disobedient. But God never makes us obey. He gives us the choice to cross over or not. Today, refuse to quit. Grab what's yours, feed your fear to the pigs, and then cross over to the other side to find your pearl of wisdom.

Whether you are scared or not, you must realize that God would not have you do something you cannot handle. —Michelle, 28

It's hard to come to the point where you understand that God allows trials to refine and perfect you. Personally, I truly believe if God didn't allow trials in my life, I would have rebelled against Him a long time ago. Anxiety keeps me humble and shows me my need for Him.

I want you to know, dear friend, that you are not alone. Today, if you're struggling with crossing to the other side, if you're struggling with the idea of forgiveness, ask God to replace your anxiety with His perfect peace (Isaiah 26:3).

Luke 18:40-41 says, "When Jesus heard him, he stopped and ordered that the man be brought to him. As the man came near, Jesus asked him, 'What do you want me to do for you?'" What is one thing you need Jesus to do for you? Is there anything hindering you from crying out to the Lord as the blind man did?

First Samuel 1:11 says, "LORD Almighty, if you will only look on your servant's misery and remember me, and not forget your servant but give her a son, then I will give him to the LORD for all the days of his life, and no razor will ever be used on his head." Have you ever tried to make a deal with God? What was the outcome?

Job 2:13 says, "Then they sat on the ground with him for seven days and seven nights. No one said a word to him, because they saw how great his suffering was." Have you ever felt like you've suffered enough? What made you feel that way and why?

Read the parable of the Pharisee and the tax collector in **Luke 18:9-14.** Have you ever thought your faith was better than someone else's? Is there anyone in particular you can think of that you need to apologize to because of this? Or have you ever felt like you weren't worthy of being forgiven or being God's child because of something you said or did?

Isaiah 43:1 says "Do not fear, for I have redeemed you; I have summoned you by name; you are mine." Can you remember a time when you knew that God had brought you out of the prison of your sin by forgiving you?

Second Corinthians 2:5,7 says, "If anyone has caused you grief... you ought to forgive and comfort him, so that he will not be overwhelmed by excessive sorrow." Have you waited too long to forgive someone—or to ask someone to forgive you? Write a prayer asking God for the courage today to speak up.

Psalm 56:1 says, "Be merciful to me, my God, for my enemies are in hot pursuit; all day long they press their attack." Has anyone judged you too harshly? How did it make you feel? How does it change the way you judge others?

Read the story of Jesus being anointed by a sinful woman in **Luke 7:36-50**. Have you ever struggled to believe that God removes your sin "as far as the east is from the west"? If so, why?

James 1:12 says, "Blessed is the one who perseveres under trial because, having stood the test, that person will receive the crown of life that the Lord has promised to those who love him." Have you ever been afraid to cross over to the other side? Write a prayer asking God to give you the courage to face a person, place, or thing that troubles you.

CHAPTER 7

Intended for Good

In this book so far I have mentioned many different ways to forgive and be forgiven. Here comes the hard part! *Reconciliation*. What is standing in the way? What's preventing you from forgiving and being reconciled? Maybe you have forgiven the person who offended you in your heart, but you're struggling to regain trust in the relationship. Maybe the relationship is over and you're left with the broken pieces. Or let's be honest—maybe you don't *want* to reconcile.

I found an interesting point of view on Voice of the Martyrs' blog while researching this last possibility. It goes like this:

> An American man and his five-year-old son came up to meet the North Korean after his presentation, and the American greeted our brother by saying, "This is my son, Little Timmy. He prays every night that God will open Kim Jong Il's heart to accept the gospel."
>
> Our North Korean brother turned to us and said, "Really? I just pray every night that God kills him."
>
> Yes, beautiful, breathtaking forgiveness does happen among persecuted Christians. But it happens among those who have daily kept their hearts tender before the Lord

through far less breathtaking, far more mundane acts of forgiveness preceding the hurt. The most moving stories of forgiveness in places like North Korea and Pakistan and Eritrea are not ones where a persecuted Christian spontaneously extends forgiveness to those who harmed his family.[1]

Chances are if you live in the United States, you're not persecuted for your faith. There's no possibility of jail time in your future because of your faith. However, you might be confused as to *why* you're still suffering. I also understand that even under the most extreme conditions forgiveness *and* reconciliation are possible with God. What the enemy intends for harm God can use for good (Genesis 50:20).

Do you remember the story of Joseph? He suffered terribly at the hands of those closest to him—his brothers. Can you imagine being shoved down into a pit, being sold into slavery, and thinking you'd never see your father again? Before I get into his story, I want you to see that twice in the Bible we're told to not be surprised *when* we suffer—not if. We are told to rejoice and be blessed. Excuse me, but how exactly does that work?

> Consider it pure joy, my brothers and sisters, whenever you face trials of many kinds, because you know that the testing of your faith develops perseverance. Let perseverance finish its work so that you may be mature and complete, not lacking anything (James 1:2-4).

> If you are insulted because of the name of Christ, you are blessed, for the Spirit of glory and of God rests on you (1 Peter 4:14).

It's difficult to consider suffering as a blessing, especially if we've done nothing wrong. As I've shared before, I grew up in a Christian home. I never seriously rebelled. I was the good girl. I never went through a party phase, did drugs, or slept around. I thought I was doing everything God asked me too…and yet I suffered. *Big time.*

It's only when we look to God, the author and perfecter of our faith, and cry out for His help that He *frees* us. It might not be in that moment, and there might still be a long road ahead. But God knows better. *That* is the reason why God can get glory. Every time.

Yes—suffering for doing right is just plain awful. Maybe you don't understand what is happening to you. Maybe like me, you can't see changes up ahead. Maybe you're discouraged and the last thing you feel right now is *blessed*. But there is a way out. Today, if you are suffering for doing what is right, know that you are *blessed*. Jesus said so during the Sermon on the Mount: "Blessed are those who are persecuted because of righteousness, for theirs is the kingdom of heaven" (Matthew 5:10).

> Always remember that Jesus Christ...was raised from the dead. This is the Good News I preach. And because I preach this Good News, I am suffering and have been chained like a criminal. But the word of God cannot be chained. So I am willing to endure anything if it will bring salvation and eternal glory in Christ Jesus to those God has chosen (2 Timothy 2:8-10 NLT).

I think a big part of forgiveness is overlooked when taught in church, and that's the trust aspect. I'm reminded of this when looking at the story of Joseph. He forgave his brothers but did not immediately reveal himself. He tested them first to see if they had changed, and once he had ascertained that they were different he gave them his trust again. If this had been taught more in church it would have saved me a lot of emotional pain. —Ashlie, 24

Strong Enough to Forgive

The movie *As We Forgive* chronicles the lives of two survivors of the chilling Rwandan genocide. It's pretty intense to watch each of them meet the man who killed their families. One of them forgives right away because she knows it's the right thing to do. The other doesn't. She can't. She's paralyzed by fear, hatred, and who knows what else!

While watching the movie, you have to ask yourself, *Would I be strong enough to forgive someone like that?* Doesn't it just put forgiveness into perspective? It's not like someone murdered *my* husband and children, leaving me on the side of the road to die in their blood.

The story of Rwanda just makes my heart bleed. But there's beauty right alongside the pain. The government of Rwanda created an opportunity for the murderers to build houses for the survivors of the genocide. The movie also shows local pastors aiding in the process of reconciliation because of the sensitivity of the project. It's almost chilling to watch.

The most touching part about the movie was the woman who struggled to forgive the man who killed her family. Yes, the pastor encouraged her in every way possible. Yes, the man built her a home. It wasn't until after the village stepped in to help her move all of her things—including her crops, which was the only thing she could survive on—that she gave in. It took an entire village to bring redemption to just one woman. The transformation in her heart is amazing. She was able to provide for one more season, but she also received the most precious gift of all. *Freedom.* She found freedom by forgiving the man who had ruined her life.

I'm still hurt, confused, and scared to approach my situation. I like to believe I have a strong faith, but if I'm unable to forgive myself and others, is it really strong? —Amber, 26

I struggle with my failed relationships. Fear has prevented me from taking new opportunities. —Jocelyn, 27

Her eyes light up when she tells the story. Before she sat limp and lifeless, and now she talks boldly and without shame. I encourage you to watch the movie if you're struggling, and be amazed at the capacity of the human heart to forgive.

But let's get back to the story of Joseph. His brothers told their father that he'd been killed, disguising the truth. They'd sold him for twenty pieces of silver (which was actually the price paid for a handicapped slave in those days) to Midianite traders they happened to see coming their way. Sometimes the people who hurt you the most are those to whom you are closest, like your best friends or family members. Look at Joseph. He opened his heart to his brothers. He shared his hopes and dreams. *Literally.* His brothers were jealous of him and the extra attention he got from their father. They hated him. So they sold Joseph into slavery (Genesis 37:28).

Lost and Found

Do you remember the television show *Lost*? It's one of my favorites. I used to turn my phone on silent and log off the internet completely to watch the show, which says a lot if you know me! The script, the plot, the characters, and the location were all incredible. I found it fascinating that this group of people came together so quickly through such a traumatic trial.

I found it interesting to watch the flashbacks of the characters before Oceanic Flight 815 crashed on a mysterious island. They were already lost. Although none of them knew it, the island brought them a new level of redemption. Community. Hope in chaos.

That's what we are to each other.

That's what the story of Joseph proves. He was stuck on an "island" of his own—a prison—for 13 years! But in that time God taught him and groomed him for the position he would hold someday as Pharaoh's right-hand man. Joseph was lost, and it took isolation in a prison for him to find his true worth.

Life is a pressure force. We're all striving for performance. Anything that enhances our pathetic little lives. We feel lost when we don't know how to get where we want to go. Scared. Sometimes it takes a major event to get our attention—like a plane crash, the death of a loved one, or an unplanned pregnancy. Until we come to grips with who we truly are and Whose we are we will continue to walk in darkness.

But it's the weirdest thing. After death comes life. After the storm comes the Son. After forgiveness comes reconciliation. The past ten years of my life constantly serve as my daily reminder of the cross. Let's seek forgiveness from our past and watch as Jesus finds us in the present—and transforms our hopes for the future. We're no longer lost.

The Greater Good

At the time of our troubles we cannot see God shaping and molding us for the future. We're focused on the fact that we've been sold (like Jacob) or stranded (like the characters in *Lost*). Good riddance! No more lookin' back! Today is the day to move forward into the future. No more dwelling on all those troubles because God, our lifeline, has never let us go. He knows what will bring the greatest good out of our lives. We can praise Him for allowing a deeper work in us. Yes, this anguish was worthwhile. Maybe it was even *good*.

Can you say that?

When you struggle through trials it may feel like you'll never stop crying. It's easy for our fears to overtake us. We might struggle with the thought, *I'll be stuck forever.*

You may not see God working on your behalf, but He is. King David wrote,

> I used to wander off until you disciplined me;
> but now I closely follow your word...
> My suffering was good for me,
> for it taught me to pay attention to your decrees
> (Psalm 119:67,71 NLT).

David learned the principle of the greater good. Even I have learned to pay attention through my trials. Ask God to teach you what He wants you to learn so He can either take the trial away or teach you and make you stronger because of it.

Joseph is a great biblical example of the greater good. Here is his story. I know it's long, but I hope you'll stay with me as I present the highlights. Later, on your own, I encourage you on your own time to read through Genesis 37–50 with a pen and a journal and ask God to speak to you.

Joseph's Story

Joseph was the son of Jacob and Rachel. He had one full brother, Benjamin, and ten stepbrothers—Reuben, Simeon, Levi, Judah, Issachar, Zebulun, Dan, Naphtali, Gad, and Asher.

Joseph was the favorite of all twelve sons of Jacob and was given a richly ornamented robe. His brothers hated him for being the favorite, for bringing a bad report about their work in the field, and because he didn't have to lift a finger.

Joseph had two dreams in which his brothers bowed down before him, which caused his brothers to resent him even to the point of killing him. But Reuben convinced the brothers not to kill Joseph. Judah had the idea to sell Joseph into slavery. A group of Midianite merchants paid twenty shekels of silver for Joseph and took him to Egypt.

But the brothers needed a convincing story for their father. Joseph's brothers tore his robe and splattered it with goat's blood, then told Jacob that an animal had attacked and killed Joseph.

The Midianites sold Joseph to a man named Potiphar in Egypt. Potiphar was one of Pharaoh's officials, the captain of the guard. The Lord was with Joseph and Potiphar put Joseph in charge of his entire household and everything he owned.

Joseph was "well-built and handsome" (Genesis 39:6), and Potiphar's wife tried to get Joseph to sleep with her. Many times she begged and each time he refused. One day she grabbed him by his cloak to try to seduce him. He ran away...but left his cloak in her hand. So what did Potiphar's wife do? She accused Joseph of trying to rape her.

Instead of a death sentence, Potiphar threw Joseph in prison. But the Lord was with Joseph in prison and the prison warden put him in charge of everything.

One night two of Pharaoh's prisoners had dreams and weren't sure what they meant. Joseph interpreted them with God's help and they both came true. One of the prisoners was executed and one was restored to his position of honor. Joseph asked this second prisoner, Pharaoh's cupbearer, to help save him, but the man forgot him.

Two years passed. Then, one night, Pharaoh had two dreams that deeply disturbed him. The cupbearer remembered Joseph's ability to interpret dreams. Joseph was brought up from prison, and with God's help he interpreted Pharaoh's dreams. A terrible famine was coming.

Pharaoh was so impressed that he put Joseph in charge of all of Egypt, making him second-in-command only to himself. And it was a good thing he put Joseph in charge, because the famine came just as the dream had foretold. Harvests were bad all over—not just in Egypt. The famine forced Joseph's stepbrothers to journey from Canaan to Egypt to buy grain. They bowed before Joseph and did not recognize him. But Joseph recognized his brothers and tested them to see if they had changed. He took Simeon and had him bound and put in prison in front of his brothers. He also told them not to come back without Benjamin.

Jacob nearly had a heart attack when he heard what happened to his sons in Egypt. He refused to let them go back because Benjamin was now his favored son and God forbid anything would happen to him. But finally the famine became so severe that Jacob had to let Benjamin go back with the rest of his brothers.

Finally, Joseph revealed himself to his brothers. He wept, telling his brothers…

> Do not be distressed and do not be angry with yourselves for selling me here, because it was to save lives that God sent me ahead of you. For two years now there has been famine in the land, and for the next five years there will be no plowing and reaping. But God sent me ahead of you to preserve for you a remnant on earth and to save your lives by a great deliverance. So then, it was not you who sent me here, but God (Genesis 45:5-8).

Joseph moved his entire family from Canaan to Egypt, where he could provide for them. He told his brothers, "You intended to harm me, but God intended it for good to accomplish what is now being done, the saving of many lives" (Genesis 50:20). In his book *Joseph: A Man of Integrity and Forgiveness*, Charles Swindoll says, "I am confident that every time they went back and started to rehearse their wrongs, Joseph stopped them. 'We're not going there. That was then, this is now. God had a plan and it's all worked out for our good and His glory. Let's talk about that.'"[2]

When it comes down to it, the only things that last are your relationships with other people and God. It can be really lame, but things do happen for a reason and difficult times are when you really see who you are because God strips everything else away...It can be a minute-to-minute thing to hold yourself together, and that is where you need to lean on God and cling to his promises. — Angela, 28

Forgive First, Trust Later

Joseph didn't just forgive his brothers. He put the past behind him and decided to become a part of the family again. He *trusted* his brothers.

Thank God Joseph didn't just throw his brothers in prison when they traveled to Egypt to buy grain from him—otherwise we wouldn't get to see them reconcile.

It's interesting that he waited to tell them who he was. Maybe Joseph needed more information. He needed to know if their father was still alive. He also wanted to see Benjamin. Without knowing to whom they were speaking, the brothers told Joseph all about his family and then some.

He tested them.

He asked them questions. He didn't just blindly offer his forgiveness right away. Joseph wanted to see if they were ready to hear the truth before he revealed who he was to them. If you think about it, the story of Joseph is even more meaningful to us and to his brothers because they were found *not guilty*.

Next time you're searching for truth and how to forgive others who have harmed you—remember forgiveness is freely given, but trust is earned.

But God!

When I was reading through the story of Joseph I didn't find any verse or sentence that said how Joseph was angry, upset, or wanted revenge. Instead, we find something even more remarkable: The Lord was with Joseph.

> The Lord was with Joseph so that he prospered, and he lived in the house of his Egyptian master. When his master saw that the Lord was with him and that the Lord gave him success in everything he did, Joseph found favor in his eyes and became his attendant. Potiphar put him in charge of his household, and he entrusted to his care everything he owned. From the time he put him in charge of his household and of all that he owned, the Lord blessed the household of the Egyptian because of Joseph. The blessing of the Lord was on everything Potiphar had, both in the house and in the field. So Potiphar left everything he had in Joseph's care; with Joseph in charge, he did not concern himself with anything except the food he ate (Genesis 39:2-6).

As Charles Swindoll puts it, "Joseph didn't have to tell Potiphar that the Lord was with him; Potiphar could see it for himself."[3]

You would think the life of a slave would be a miserable one. I'm assuming Joseph thought his life would be wretched because he was sold by his brothers for the price of a handicapped slave—just twenty pieces of silver. *Yikes.* I bet that would make you or me think twice about our worth, but it doesn't even faze Joseph. Somehow his work ethic (who knew he had one, since his father never made him work) combined with the Lord's help was so impressive that Potiphar put him in charge of his entire household!

Somehow, Joseph doesn't seem like much of a slave anymore. He's second-in-command to the Captain of the Guard. Even so, God allowed Joseph to learn how to serve others first before reuniting him with his family. Maybe it was God's way of testing Joseph to see if he was ready to handle the enormous task He was about to reveal.

And then there was Potiphar's wife. Poor Joseph. He might have thought his life was over *again*, but he couldn't yet see God setting key people and places behind the scenes for him to take over as second-in-command to Pharaoh himself, overseeing the livelihood of all of Egypt.

> But while Joseph was there in the prison, the LORD was with him; he showed him kindness and granted him favor in the eyes of the prison warden. So the warden put Joseph in charge of all those held in the prison, and he was made responsible for all that was done there. The warden paid no attention to anything under Joseph's care, because the LORD was with Joseph and gave him success in whatever he did (Genesis 39:20-23).

And then there was the cupbearer. Joseph interpreted a dream for him and the baker. Both dreams were fulfilled just as Joseph said. The cupbearer was restored to his royal position while the baker was put to death. But just as quickly as he was released from prison, the cupbearer forgot about Joseph (Genesis 40:23). So close and yet so far.

Have you been there? You come so close to forgiving someone or get your hopes up…only to find yourself back behind the same prison bars.

But I want to point out something interesting. After eleven years of slavery, many of them spent in prison, Joseph wasn't holding on to any bitterness. If he had, there is no way he would have noticed the cupbearer was sad in the first place. You would think every day in prison is a sad day, right? *Wrong!* Not with Joseph.

> When Joseph came to them the next morning, he saw that they were dejected. So he asked Pharaoh's officials who were in custody with him in his master's house, "Why do you look so sad today?" (Genesis 40:6).

If you're anything like me, when you're going through a stressful situation you definitely don't tend to notice others around you who are simply *sad*. You have no time. You're too busy nursing your own wounds to think of someone else's boo-boo.

Because Joseph was free of bitterness he could interpret others' dreams even before his came true. All too often in America we're too concerned with our own dreams.

- The dream of an education
- The dream of the perfect relationship
- The dream of owning a house and having children, a white picket fence, and a dog
- The dream of climbing the corporate ladder
- The dream of perfect health
- The dream of having no debt and driving a sports car

You name it, Americans have dreamt it. Maybe you're wondering when the God of Justice will come in and sweep you off your feet, away from all the strife, so you can get on with your life and *your* dream. Maybe you're waiting for your future spouse, sick of always being the bridesmaid. *Have no fear!* The God of Mercy and Justice not only sees you—He *knows*. His timing is impeccable. He will not delay.

After Death Comes Life!

God's promises never come up short. But how many of us act like we believe them? How many of us act like we still have hope? One of my all-time favorite devotionals, *Streams in the Desert*, says this about God's promises:

> We need to be more businesslike and use common sense with God in claiming His promises. If a man were to go to the bank several times a day, lay his check at the teller's window, and then pick it up and leave without cashing it, it would not be long before the bank would have him ordered from the premises. People who go to the bank have a purpose in mind. They present their check, receive their cash, and then leave, having transacted real business.[4]

It's easy to become ashamed of your chronic sufferings that seem to have no end in sight. You might feel like a freak, going to the bank of God over and over again. Nobody likes to appear weak. We like to hide our panic attacks. Sometimes we need the perspective of Joseph. That's why I shared his story at such length and in as much detail. Joseph had to wait thirteen years before God fulfilled his childhood dream. I, too, at the young age of fifteen knew one day God would bring me a husband. I had no idea, however, that I would have to wait twelve years, ten months, and twenty-four days for Marc to propose and ask me to be his wife.

That's a lot of waiting.

Maybe for you it's five years, two months, and twenty-three days for you. Maybe you've lost count. Maybe you never counted. Thankfully, Joseph did not waste any time letting God use him…whether he was in a mansion, stuck in prison, or in the palace of Pharaoh.

Can the same be said of you?

Yes, the message of the cross is real. Yes, there's pain, but there is also the joy of resurrection.

Your body may feel wretched. Maybe you even smell the stench of Satan. You know deep down in your heart that you must go back to the place where discouragement happened. Like Joseph, you must face the person or people who hurt you. You need to forgive those who harmed you. Maybe not today, but one day. In the midnight hour, when darkness circles around you, it's okay to sit down in distress and weep with heavy sobs. God can handle your situation, just like He handled Joseph's. Through the message of the cross we can give up control for the future we wanted.

In our sufferings, we have the awesome privilege of identifying with Jesus. Once we take up our cross we find hope. It's amazing how one act of surrender, submission, and humility can help us regain control. Giving up doesn't mean you're a failure. It gives God the ability to do what He already said He'd do—*take over.* God can and will use everything the enemy intended to harm you for His good. Today you have the choice to get alone with God and conduct business. Pray. Get on your knees. Read the Word. Worship. Take a walk.

Are you listening?

You can trust Him when you're faced with the deepest, darkest night of the soul. Say this out loud with me:

I refuse to allow my disbelief, pain, and the horror of the present to cause me to doubt. After death comes life! There is hope in Jesus.

Genesis 45:5 says, "Do not be distressed and do not be angry with yourselves for selling me here, because it was to save lives that God sent me ahead of you." Write a prayer asking for God to give you His perspective on the suffering you're currently experiencing.

Genesis 50:20 says, "You intended to harm me, but God intended it for good to accomplish what is now being done, the saving of many lives." Describe a time when, looking back, you've been able to see a larger purpose in your suffering.

Romans 8:38-39 says, "I am convinced that neither death nor life, neither angels nor demons, neither the present nor the future, nor any powers, neither height nor depth, nor anything else in all creation, will be able to separate us from the love of God that is in Christ Jesus our Lord." What makes you feel lost, apart from God? Write down anything that you feel currently distracts you or separates you from His love.

Isaiah 38:17 says, "Surely it was for my benefit that I suffered such anguish. In your love you kept me from the pit of destruction; you have put all my sins behind your back." How has God used your trials for good? Do you feel you're a stronger person because of them?

Take some time to read the story of Joseph in **Genesis 37–50.** Is there any bitterness that you are still holding on to? Anyone you haven't yet forgiven or reconciled with? Any dreams that you feel you're still waiting on? Write down a prayer to God. Confess your sins and ask God to give you the courage to keep waiting no matter how long it takes—even if it takes thirteen years.

Discussion Questions

Chapter 1

1. Could you forgive a man who murdered twelve people and wounded fifty-eight more? Why or why not?

2. Write down a list of *what ifs* and give them over to God. Discuss them in your small group to see if there is a common thread such as irrational fears or unforgiveness.

3. If forgiveness is the key, then how come you and I have such a hard time letting go? What would it take for you to finally let it go?

4. Read aloud the transformative prayer by Neil T. Anderson together and discuss with your small group.

5. Does forgiveness intimidate you? Should it? Why or why not?

6. Do you think it's possible to fight sin instead of attacking each other?

Chapter 2

1. Is it easier to hide your sins or come clean and ask for forgiveness? Why?

2. Do you need lots of alone time to process? Or do you process situations quickly? Knowing what kind of processor you are will help you as you learn how to forgive others—including yourself.

3. Have you ever been robbed of the opportunity to forgive and reconcile with someone who hurt you? What do you think God is calling you to do about that particular situation and why?

4. Have you ever felt God couldn't forgive you for any reason?

5. Review the acrostic for C-H-R-I-S-T on page 47. Look up the verses and discuss them together in your small group.

Chapter 3

1. Has God ever told you *no*? What were the circumstances and the final outcome?

2. Have you ever lashed out *about* a person to someone who you knew would sympathize and agree with your side of the story? Why do you think it's easy to do so?

3. Look at the C.S. Lewis quotation on page 62. Do you agree with this statement? Why or why not?

4. Was there ever a time when you ever demanded God to answer you like Job? Why or why not?

5. Was there a time when you asked God (like Abraham) to bless you? If so, share the situation with your small group.

6. Page 68 includes a prayer of forgiveness for oneself. Read it aloud with your small group and discuss your struggles in this area.

Chapter 4

1. Like Jonah, have you ever had a hard time forgiving someone even after God already has?

2. If you were to make a list of people who've offended you, who would be on it and why? What is holding you back from forgiving those people?

3. Have you ever "ripped someone a new one?" Did you feel better? Or did you regret your words?

4. What would cause you to withhold forgiveness? Would it be a particular sin or a particular person? Why?

5. Do you have a hard time moving forward from your mistakes? Why or why not?

6. Are you suffering as a result of another person's sin? Reread page 97 if so.

Chapter 5

1. Is God disciplining you? Pruning you? Asking you to remain in forgiveness? Read John 15 with your small group and discuss its implications for your life and situation.

2. Have you ever been disappointed by unmet expectations?

3. Was there ever a time in your life when forgiveness (or the lack of it) affected more than your relationships? (Your opportunities? Your work? Your outlook on life? Your future?)

4. Do you have the courage to forgive the person who hurt you the most?

5. Have you ever tried treating the symptoms of unforgiveness instead of getting to the root of the problem? How far did that get you? Why do you think that is?

Chapter 6

1. In what kinds of ways have you seen Jesus set others free?

2. Read Ava Pennington's quotation on page 134. Is intercessory prayer connected to forgiveness? Why or why not?

3. Describe a time when God changed your heart toward another person.

4. Is forgiveness a gift? Why or why not?

5. Have you ever compared your trials to the trials of others? How did it make you feel and why?

6. Do you believe forgiveness erases the past? Why or why not?

Chapter 7

1. What's the difference between forgiveness and reconciliation? Is one harder than the other?

2. Do you believe "it takes a village" to forgive?

3. Genesis never mentions Joseph being angry, upset, or wanting revenge. Why do you think this is?

4. Have you come close to forgiving someone only to find yourself unable to go through with it?

5. What has God taught you about forgiveness after reading through this book?

ACKNOWLEDGMENTS

To Jesus, Who has made me *fruitful* in the land of my sufferings (Genesis 41:52).

To Ericka, whom God used to tell me many, many years ago to write a book on suffering.

To my family, who helped me through the toughest years of my life.

To my amazing team at Harvest House Publishers, for not letting my dream of writing a book on forgiveness die, and giving me the chance to write my first non-devotional book.

To my husband, Marc—I couldn't have finished this book without your love and support.

To everyone who took my survey—I appreciate your quotes. Thanks for allowing me to share your stories in this book.

To Star the pit bull—Thanks for being such a great writing dog.

Renee Fisher, the Devotional Diva®, is the spirited speaker and author of *Faithbook of Jesus, Not Another Dating Book, Forgiving Others, Forgiving Me,* and *Loves Me Not.* A graduate of Biola University, Renee's mission in life is to "spur others forward" (Hebrews 10:24) using the lessons learned from her own trials to encourage others in their walk with God. She and her husband, Marc, live in California with their dog, Rock Star. Learn more about Renee at **www.devotionaldiva.com.**

Notes

Chapter 1

1. Neil. T. Anderson, *Steps to Freedom in Christ* (La Habra, CA: Freedom in Christ Youth Ministries, 1994), 2.
2. Billy Graham, *Unto the Hills* (Nashville: Thomas Nelson, 2010), August 10.
3. Brad Strait, "A Miracle Inside the Aurora Shooting: One Victim's Story," *Celtic Straits* (blog), July 22, 2012, http://bstrait.wordpress.com/2012/07/22/a-miracle-inside-the-aurora-shooting-one-victims-story/.

Chapter 2

1. Charles Ringma, *Seize the Day with Dietrich Bonhoeffer* (Colorado Springs: NavPress, 2000), June 27.

Chapter 3

1. Charles Ringma, *Seize the Day with Dietrich Bonhoeffer* (Colorado Springs: NavPress, 2000), August 2.
2. C.S. Lewis, *A Grief Observed* (New York: HarperCollins, 2002), 43.

Chapter 4

1. Kay Arthur, *Lord, Heal My Hurts* (Colorado Springs: WaterBrook Press, 1998), 181.
2. Billy Graham, *Unto the Hills* (Nashville: Thomas Nelson, 2010), January 29.
3. Neil. T. Anderson, *Steps to Freedom in Christ* (La Habra, CA: Freedom in Christ Youth Ministries, 1994), 1.
4. Nancy Leigh DeMoss, *Brokenness* (Chicago: Moody Publishers, 2002), 37.
5. L.B. Cowman, *Streams in the Desert* (Grand Rapids, MI: Zondervan, 1996), June 19.
6. Bruce Wilkinson, *Secrets of the Vine* (Sisters, OR: Multnomah Press, 2001), 57-58.
7. Pastor Chris Brown, "The Long Road Home" (sermon, North Coast Church, Vista, CA, August 15, 2010).

Chapter 5

1. Bruce Wilkinson, *Secrets of the Vine* (Sisters, OR: Multnomah Press, 2001), 74.
2. Joanna Weaver, *Lazarus Awakening* (Colorado Springs: WaterBrook Press, 2011), 148.
3. Ibid.

Chapter 6

1. Ava Pennington, *One Year Alone with God* (Grand Rapids, MI: Revell, 2010), 249.

2. Neil T. Anderson, *The Bondage Breaker* (Eugene, OR: Harvest House, 1990), 195.

3. Gary Chapman, *The Five Love Languages* (Chicago: Northfield Publishing, 1992), 143.

Chapter 7

1. "Persecuted Christians Struggle with Unforgiveness, Too," *The Voice of the Martyrs* (blog), August 28, 2012, http://vomcblog.blogspot.com/2012/08/persecuted-christians-struggle-with.html.

2. Charles R. Swindoll, *Joseph: A Man of Integrity and Forgiveness* (Nashville: Thomas Nelson, 1998), 147.

3. Ibid., 24.

4. L.B. Cowman, *Streams in the Desert* (Grand Rapids, MI: Zondervan, 1996), April 6.

NOT ANOTHER DATING BOOK

A Devotional Guide to All Your Relationships
By Renee Fisher

For every twenty-something who's thrown aside traditional relationship books in despair comes a new kind of dating book. Renee Fisher,
a refreshing new voice for today's generation, pulls no punches as she
addresses the real, relevant questions and issues young adults encoun-
ter today:

- How do I honor God with my body?
- What's the deal with online dating?
- Does it matter if my significant other is a Christian?
- Is there only one person out there for me?
- Can God use me in my singleness?
- How should I relate to my ex after a breakup?
- I think there's more to life than dating—but what?
- What happens if I've made mistakes?

With her trademark wit and enthusiasm, Renee Fisher, Devotional
Diva® and author of *Faithbook of Jesus*, urges young adults to take a
closer look at the way they relate to God and others, showing them that
every relationship finds its perfect example in Christ. Each daily devo-
tion includes scriptural insight, prayers, journaling space, and questions
for further thought from real-life twenty-somethings.

CALLED TO STAY

An Uncompromising Mission to Save Your Church
By Caleb Breakey

The Church?

Heavy on tradition but light on conviction.
Overflowing with knowledge but dry in spirit.
Plenty of small talk but no real community.

...at least that's what the Millennials are saying. This generation of young adults wants to follow Christ, but many don't see any need for the Church in that equation.

Enter breakout new author Caleb Jennings Breakey. In his debut book, Caleb encourages young people not to abandon the church, but to put their passion to use for the church. Caleb shows his generation how to

- inject truth, passion, and conviction into other believers
- live as a reflection of Jesus, both in and out of the church
- contribute to the solution instead of giving up

The church desperately needs Millennials who are passionate for Christ, hungry for the Word, humble in all things, and fearless in spurring on the body of Christ to love and good works. The Millennials have the passion. Caleb Jennings Breakey will show them how to use it.

WHY CAN'T WE JUST GET ALONG?

6 Effective Skills for Dealing with Difficult People

By Shelley Hendrix

Every woman suffers from relationships that seem broken and past the point of salvaging. *Why Can't We Just Get Along?* provides a warm, friendly, and candid resource for women to look honestly at relationship issues and take control of their own lives…regardless of the choices others make. Author and speaker Shelley Hendrix unpacks six biblical principles that will enable readers to "be at peace with everyone."

With practical, easy-to-understand tools, Shelley helps women

- find peace in their lives and friendships
- discover new motivation to restore and repair hurting relationships
- create closer connections by accepting and appreciating differences in others
- become empowered to serve each other in love

Complete with discussion questions, real-life illustrations, teaching from Scripture, and expert advice from psychologists and therapists, *Why Can't We Just Get Along?* is an invaluable resource for women everywhere, showing them how to find peace in places they never thought they could.

Helpful Scriptures

Ever wonder how to forgive? The Bible is full of stories that show you just what real forgiveness looks like and teach you how to forgive those who have wronged you—even if that person is yourself. Below is a list of all the verses I gathered in this book. Do not be afraid to find each verse in your Bible and mark it up. Maybe God will say something new to you through Scripture. And remember: *Do not fear*. God has your back and He will help you journey through the valley of unforgiveness up to the mountaintop of peace.

Genesis
15:2
17:18
37:28
39:2-6
39:20-23
4:7
40:6
40:23
45:5
50:20

Numbers
32:5

Deuteronomy
8:5

Joshua
7

1 Samuel
1:11
15:10-25

2 Samuel
12:1-13

1 Kings
18:21
19

2 Kings
13

Job
1:21-22
2:9
2:13
30:27
38:2
40:4

Job
42:1-5
42:6
42:7-9

Psalms
4:4
17:6
23:4
25:3
28:7
40:2
46:10
51:4
56:1
66:18-20
103:12
119:67, 71
139:23

Proverbs
3:11-12
4:23
4:25-27
12:1
12:19
17:9
26:11

Isaiah
1:18
26:3
29:16
30:15-16
38:17
43:1
43:19
45:24
54:17
55:8-9

Jeremiah
17:9

Lamentations
3:22-24

Ezekiel
36:26

Daniel
3:15-18

Hosea
6:1-39

Jonah
1:3
3:4

Matthew
5:10
5:22-24
5:44
6:14-15
6:33
8:28-34
10:39
11:25
18:12
18:15
18:21-35
19:14
26:75

Mark
9:24

Luke
2:46,49
7:36-50
17:3-4
18:9-14
18:35-43

John
1:12
4:14
8:3-11
8:36
8:44
9:1-7
10:10
15:1-17
21:15-19

Acts
2:38
3:6
9:1
9:3-4
15:26
17:11
18:13-16

Romans
3:23
4:20-22
5:3-4
8:1-2
8:26-27
8:28
8:35

Romans
8:37-39
12:1-2
15:1

1 Corinthians
3:9
3:13
13:5
15:9-10

2 Corinthians
1:2-7
2:5,7
2:14-17
10:4
10:5
11:30
12:9-10

Ephesians
1:1
1:3
1:7
2:4-5
2:8-9
3:12
6:11-17

Philippians
2:6
2:12-13
3:5-10
4:19

Colossians
2:10
3:13

2 Timothy
1:7
2:8-10
3:16

Hebrews
6:19
10:30
10:35-36
12:1-2
13:8

James
1:2-4
1:12
1:21
5:13-16
5:19-20

1 Peter
4:15
5:7
5:8

1 John
1:9
3:19-20
4:18-20

Revelation
3:19